My Way ....

The Journey hOMe

Ocean Melchizedek

My Way Zen

Cover image
The cover image for the book is based on the Zen circle, ⁽円相⁾Ensō.

Contact details
If you have any comments on the book for the author, please email mywayzen@gmail.com.
Website: www.mywayzen.wildapricot.org

Version and copyright
1st Edition – version 2

Self-published on Kindle (KDP)

Copyright © 2019 Ocean Melchizedek. All rights reserved. No part of this publication may be reproduced, stored in a retrieval system, or transmitted, in any form or by any means without the prior written permission of the author.

ISBN
ISBN: 978-1-729-25602-2

Sponsored by the OM Peace Foundation

Foreword

The Zen of Ocean Melchizedek

This book combines the story of my personal journey on the spiritual path with information about the Great Solar Flash ("GSF"). The GSF is perhaps the most important part of this book. It is my belief, backed by science and prophecy, that we are on the Ascension timeline gifted to us by the Sun. I have an extremely positive view on what this will mean for us, or rather for some of us. There is always free choice and some beings may choose to experience the destructive aspects of the GSF. The main purpose of writing this book is to alert you to the GSF and offer suggestions as to what to do about it.

The book contains many ideas associated with different religions, but I hope the reader will see that the way forward is to go beyond religion and other dogmatic belief systems to a universal way of seeing the world. I have used religious sounding words in the book such as God, the Divine, the Kingdom, Ascension and so on, but what I am trying to point to is inexpressible in words. It takes the "Zen like" position of going beyond thought forms and rigid beliefs, to see the ultimate truth behind the words.

In writing this book, I am not trying to change anybody's beliefs or sit in judgement. The information provided here is just my take on what may be happening now and what to do about it.

My journey

I was interested in Zen from quite early on in my life. At around 40, I was introduced to the amazing trilogy of books on Zen Buddhism by DT Suzuki. Right from the first moment, I was intrigued by the stories of levitating monks and other amazing feats of Zen practitioners. I then started a formal practice of Transcendental Meditation; this was followed by Buddhism (Gelugpa, Kagyu, Nyingma and other systems); then Oneness (Oneness University and Deeksha); Shamanic practices; the I Am teachings; and finally, a return to the teachings of Jesus. For me now, my path is a unique blend of Zen, Christianity, Buddhism, New Age thought, Psychology, Shamanic practices and modern science[1]. My Way Zen is my name for this unique blending of ideas and perspectives. This name was inspired by a book called Making Zen Your Own by Janet Abels. We are all unique beings and each of us has a unique perspective on the world. Therefore, we each develop our own set of perspectives, beliefs and systems of thought. We are each at different levels of development. I am a bit of a rebel at heart and have a difficulty in conformity to a rigid set of beliefs. Zen is perfect as it has no doctrine or dogma. In fact, the opposite is true. Zen goes beyond the intellectual comings and goings of the mind and so finds the Truth.

Beyond Religion

I have tried to present the information in this book in a non-religious way. I feel religion is one of our greatest weaknesses, as it

---

[1] I use the word modern science to refer to the scientific revolution that is happening behind the scenes. The big one is the paradigm shift that sees consciousness as primary. The "material" world is secondary. The main source of the information about this paradigm shift is the Big TOE. More details about the Big TOE is in the Bibliography section at the back of this book and in chapter 2.

can so easily become fanatical with zealots willing to kill others for their "religion". Rather I suggest we go "Beyond Religion". What I mean by this will be explained later in this book.

The main sources for the information in this book are the Urantia Book[2] and the huge body of work by David Wilcock[3].

When I give talks and so on, I always explain that I do not want to change anybody's views or beliefs. Consequently, **please do your own research and come to your own conclusions about the subjects in this book.**

Fayan was one of the great Zen masters included in the book Making Zen your Own. I have included one of his famous exchanges in Appendix 3. He also wrote the 10 Admonitions to Zen teachers and students, covering laziness, poor poetry, meaningless debates and so on. If I have fallen short of any of these admonitions or made a mistake in this book, please forgive me. Any comments would be gladly welcome. Please contact me at **mywayzen@gmail.com.**

The book has lots of information and perspectives, some of which may be quite challenging. Ultimately, I don't know anything absolutely. I always leave room that I could be wrong.

The My Way Zen path is "Faith and faith alone", trusting in yourself and in the love of your God-source with gratitude. As it says in the Sufi saying: "Trust in the Lord but tether your camel

---

[2] The Urantia Book: free pdfs and audio files can be found at www.urantia.org/urantia-book/listen-urantia-book. The Urantia book contains a new revelation about the Mysteries of God, world history, Jesus and ourselves. More details can be found in the Bibliography and in Appendix 7.

[3] Books by David Wilcock include Source Field Investigations and the Ascension Mysteries. Please see Bibliography for more details.

first".

Anthropomorphic bias

You will notice in this book I'm concentrating on the ascension of humanity. The ascension is a planet wide process and involves the planetary consciousness, Gaia, her animals and plants as well as humanity. We are like flees on the back of Gaia. As she ascends, so do we.

Sequel book(s)

I plan to write a sequel to this book which will cover in more detail, many of the subjects in this book, including the global reset process. It will cover education, science, financial systems, energy, health and food systems, religions, politics, world governance and the architecture for the New Earth.

Acknowledgements

I would like to give a huge thank you to all my teachers, my parents and all the wonderful and amazing people who I have met on the path. Thank you so very much. I would particularly like to thank Rev Chris Collingwood who introduced me to a beautiful fusion of the best of Christianity with the best of Zen[4] and inspired me to write this book. In addition, I would like a big shout out to Elena, Pauline and Susan for proof reading the book.

I am indebted to David Wilcock (DW) for his amazing series of short talks on Gaia TV[5]. DW's main channel on Gaia TV is the

---

[4] Rev Chris Collingwood is the chancellor of York Minster and my Zen teacher. I am looking forward to the publication of his book whose working title is Zen Wisdom for Christians.

Wisdom Teachings but he also has another channel called Cosmic Disclosure which includes stunning revelations about the secret space program and other "secrets". These talks include testimony given by truly courageous whistle-blowers like Corey Goode, Emery Smith and others. The information on the Great Solar Flash presented in this book is largely based on the information in the talks on Gaia TV.

I am a Gemini and so I naturally seem to be able to hold many thoughts at once and see the connections between them. I hope when you read this book, it is not too overwhelming. I present a lot of information and new ideas in this book. I have tried to present them in a reasonably concise manner, as I know everyone is so busy and there is such a huge volume of data and information available to us now. This is both a boon and a curse. My solution is to present the basic ideas and provide references to the original material. If you would like to pursue any of the ideas presented here, then please feel free to access the links provided or read the books listed in the Bibliography or contact me by email. In the past I was a Chartered Accountant and have written many business type reports for management etc. I toyed with the idea of using a business style for this book, but I ended up deciding to use a chatty style as if I were having a conversation with the reader. I hope you enjoy reading the book, that it makes sense for you and gets you thinking for yourself.

My intention for this book is for it to add to the World Peace,

---

[5] Gaia TV is a paid for channel containing hundreds of videos on all sorts of topics from Yoga to Transformation, including numerous films and documentaries. There are now over 260 talks by DW on all sorts of topics ranging from the source field, geometry, ascension, DNA, the solar flash, "modern" science and much more. Apparently, Gaia TV management has been infiltrated by the Negative Agenda and DW has resigned. This does not affect DW's talks, but you need to be careful as there are a lot of false prophets and mis-information.

Harmony and Tolerance of each other with a deeper view of our place here on Earth at this time.

Ocean Melchizedek
February 2019
York and Pateley Bridge, Yorkshire.

Table of Contents

CHAPTER 1 ....**13**

    THE UNIQUE SELF 13

    MY WAY ZEN 14

    PERSONALITY 15

    NON-JUDGMENT 15

    SPIRIT AND MATTER 16

    AWAKENING 16

    YOUR SPIRITUAL PRACTICE 17

CHAPTER 2 ....**18**

    PARADIGM SHIFT IN SCIENCE..19

    HOLOGRAPHIC UNIVERSE 20

    MOVIES 20

    THE TWO AXIOMS UNDERLYING THE BIG TOE 21

    QUANTUM REALITY...23

    QUANTUM PROBABILITIES & INTENTION 24

    TIME 25

    ORGANIC OR FEELING BASED VR 27

    ARCHITECTURE 28

    OUR EXPERIENCE OF VR 29

    THE UNIVERSE AS A THOUGHT 30

    DNA 31

    QUANTUM ORGANIC VIRTUAL REALITY 32

    HACKING REALITY 32

    BASE REALITY 34

    URANTIA BOOK 35

    CYCLES OF TIME...38

    EXPERIENTIAL EVIDENCE 38

    RED PILL MOMENTS 38

    ARTIFICIAL INTELLIGENCE 40

CHAPTER 3 ....**42**

    THE GREAT SOLAR FLASH 43

    EARTH CHANGES DURING A GREAT SOLAR FLASH 44

    TIMING OF THE GSF 45

Science 45

The Harvest 46

Eschatology 48

Separation of Densities 48

Who will make it? 49

Rescue plan 49

Prophecies or Warnings 50

Solar System changes 52

Soft disclosure 54

What to do about the GSF 55

Safe Zones 55

CHAPTER 4 .... **56**

Melchizedek Lineage 56

Modern version of the Melchizedek Covenant 57

Part 1 - Quantum Virtual Reality *57*

Part 2 - God is Love *58*

Part 3 - Purification process *60*

Summary of suggested practices 61

Purification 62

Revelation 63

The Great Mystery 63

Black Belt Training 64

Melchizedek Priesthood 65

Melchizedek Teachings 65

Beyond Religion 66

Freedom and the Luciferian mistake 67

Zen Paradox 68

Freedom and surrender 68

CHAPTER 5 .... **69**

Law of attraction 71

Evolution 71

Being and Becoming 72

Diamond Light 74

Evolutionary Impulse and Desire 74

Initiations on the Christ Path 75

The New Race Genetic 77

ASCENSION GROUPS AND THE HARVEST 79

NEGATIVE AGENDA BEINGS 82

UNCONDITIONAL LOVE 82

THE JOYFUL PATH OF GOOD FORTUNE 83

CHAPTER 6 85

THE ZEN WAY HOME 85

URANTIA BOOK 86

UNITY AND THE VOID 88

KINGDOM WITHIN 89

EPILOGUE 91

BIBLIOGRAPHY 93

THE BIG TOE 93

URANTIA BOOK 93

9 KEYS 94

LAW OF ONE 94

MAKING ZEN YOUR OWN 95

SOURCE FIELD INVESTIGATIONS AND ASCENSION MYSTERIES 95

ALIEN INTERVIEW 96

THE HOLOGRAPHIC UNIVERSE 96

BIOCENTRISM 96

APPENDIX 1 – MY WAY ZEN SANGHA AND RESOURCES 98

APPENDIX 2 – ORIGINAL MELCHIZEDEK COVENANT 99

APPENDIX 3 – KOAN PRACTICE 101

APPENDIX 4 – LIST OF NAMES FOR THE "END TIMES" 103

APPENDIX 5 – MY WAY ZEN PURIFICATION 104

APPENDIX 6 – AWAKENING 127

APPENDIX 7 – THE URANTIA BOOK 129

APPENDIX 8 – FOUR BODHISATTVA VOWS 136

APPENDIX 9 – JESUS, THE MYSTERY 138

APPENDIX 10 – POLE SHIFTS 140

APPENDIX 11 – POEMS 142

APPENDIX 12 – DIAMOND LIGHT...**145**

APPENDIX 13 – THE QUEST FOR THE HOLY GRAIL.....................................**147**

APPENDIX 14 – SOURCE DECLARATION...**148**

CHAPTER 1

The Unique Self

"Always remember you are absolutely unique. Just like everyone else."
Margaret Mead

The Unique Self

The Unique Self is a simple recognition that each one of us is a unique human being. We have our own unique and sometimes complicated chain of lives and life experiences. Because each of us has a unique self, each of us has our own unique journey hOMe[6], the journey back to our source.

For the journey, we need a map. The map becomes our belief system, or religion, or the perspectives we use to navigate the world. We may call ourselves Buddhists or Christians or whatever, but when we analyse what this is, we will find we have many differences in our attitudes, morals, and beliefs, even among the same religion. Take for example Christianity. The last time I checked there were

---

[6] Home with a novel spelling. It refers to our spiritual hOMe, the Kingdom within each of us and its sound is the sound of creation - "OM".

over 3,600 different denominations or sects within Christianity. These range from the Orthodox religions such as the Greek orthodox, Russian orthodox, then there are the Roman Catholics, Jesuits and so on. Within the protestant community there are Anglicans, Methodists, Unitarians, Episcopalians, Seventh Day Adventists, Jehovah Witnesses and of course the Society of Friends or Quakers, for which I have a soft spot, having been educated at a Quaker school. Even if you belong to the same denomination, there can be many different views on many aspects of the religion. Even if the differences are small compared with the many areas where there is common ground, I contend we each have a unique take on what is true. We each have a unique system and therefore a unique religion. We are all unique beings. As the saying goes: "One Brain, One World".

My Way Zen

Our personality makes us unique. There is no-one quite like us. This is an amazing fact, and means we are all precious in the eyes of God. This miracle is the basis for the "My Way Zen" perspective: We all have a Unique Self and each one of us has a unique journey through life. I call this journey My Way Zen, as for me personally, my journey is principally a merger of two great traditions: Christianity and Buddhism (in the form of Zen). I feel closest to the Christian "thought pattern" but my version of Christianity has many additional aspects, and also a few "amendments". The main amendment is a major re-write of the Christian attitude to sin. There is sin, "missing the target", but this is not a problem for the Divine. There is no need for sacrifices or anything else similar to win God's favour. Please see the Melchizedek Covenant in Chapter 4 for an explanation of this. I would also remove all the false information about Jesus as a sacrifice.

I live in England, so my church would be the Church of England (C of E or Anglican). The beauty of this is, in the C of E, you can believe almost anything. We even had a bishop who did not believe in God[7].

Personality

The Unique Self expresses itself as personality. This is a Divine Gift. As it says in the Bible, we are made in the image of our Creator. Our Creator has personality. It is not some mindless energy. I am a big fan of the Star Wars films. In the films, the source is presented as the Force with a Light and Dark side. In my view, the Force also has personality. The personality includes the collective archetypes as revealed by Carl Jung - the Father, the Mother, the Hero and so on.

Ego mind is a key part of the personality. It gets a bad rap under some spiritual systems. For me it is neither good nor bad. It is a tool. It just has a limited perception. When your higher intelligence sees through the illusion of duality, you see the Oneness in all things and the ego is transcended.

Some aspects of Buddhism, in my view take a nihilistic view of personality. For me, it is not about self-denial but about self-acceptance, and self-validation. You have a personality, an ego and a unique self. There is no problem having an ego. Just don't let it run your life.

Non-Judgment

When you fully understand the Unique self, you can enter the

---

[7] David Jenkins, who was once bishop of Durham, was notorious for not believing in a God.

wonderful space of Non-Judgement. You realise everyone has a unique set of experiences, a unique timeline and personality. You are unable to stand in another person's shoes and therefore you cannot judge another.

Spirit and matter

The unique self is a subtle balance between Spirit and Matter. The evolutionary process could be seen as a process of spiritualising matter. One way of seeing our task here on Earth is to bring about a fusion between our spirit and material bodies. In some systems, this is seen as the need to deny the material body and its animal instincts. Life is seen as a battle between our spiritual intentions and our animal nature. For me, my advice is to embrace both.

Under the old Cartesian split, religion dealt with the spirit and science with matter. The new paradigm of modern science brings both into a unified whole. This new perspective sees consciousness as primary and the world that appears to it (i.e. you as consciousness) is therefore secondary, i.e. a virtual reality. This will be explained in more detail in the next chapter.

Awakening

For anyone starting the journey, you need to know it is a long journey, it never ends. I am still learning more and more each day and you cannot go back into a state of ignorance. If you have yet to start the journey, my challenge for you is to investigate three topics and make your own conclusions whether the "official" story is correct:

- 9/11 – Is the official story of the "terrorist" attack on the Twin Towers true?

My Way Zen

- Pyramids - were they just tombs for deceased Pharaohs?
- Why do we have 46 chromosomes, but other simians have 48, i.e. does the Darwinian evolution theory explain the source of DNA[8]?

After spending many hours investigating the above, I have arrived at some answers to the above "awakening" puzzles. These are set out at appendix 6. These are "Red Pills" (explained later in this book). If you have trouble reading this, I suggest you stop reading this book and do your own research.

Your Spiritual Practice

This whole chapter is basically an invitation to you to create your own spiritual practice. You are unique and so your spiritual practice will also be unique. It can be a mixture of different traditions, like mine. Please do your own research and feel free to borrow ideas from this book.

---

[8] You could also check where does the rhesus negative blood group come from. Approximately 15% of the population is Rhesus negative.

CHAPTER 2

Virtual Reality

"The odds that we are living in the base reality is One in Billions"
Elon Musk[9]

A key to understanding the My Way Zen path is to realise that we are living in a Virtual Reality (VR)[10]. Consciousness is primary, "matter" is basically information projected from the collective field, via our sensory organs, "onto" our consciousness. A great analogy to use for who we are in this VR is to consider your body as an avatar in a multi-player online game (MMORG) and you, as consciousness, are the player.

In this short book, I do not have time to explain the Virtual Reality theory in detail. A full explanation of this theory is brilliantly set out

---

[9] Elon Musk is the CEO of SpaceX and Tesla and is well known for his views on simulated reality.

[10] Virtual reality can also be called a simulated reality.

by Tom Campbell in his Big TOE, the Theory of Everything[11]. I thoroughly recommend watching some of the large number of YouTube videos by Tom Campbell (and others) explaining virtual reality and its application to many of life's issues.

Paradigm Shift in Science

As Tom Campbell explains, the VR theory is the next big paradigm shift in science. Many features of quantum physics are difficult to explain under the old paradigm of materialism or its modern form, physicalism. One such area is the double slit experiment[12], where the "observer" plays a key but mysterious role in the outcome. This is sometimes referred to as the "collapse of the Schrödinger wave equation". The old paradigm tries to explain consciousness as somehow emerging out of matter. Sorry guys you have it the wrong way around. Consciousness does not emerge out of matter. Rather consciousness is primary, and the world arises within it. The world is fundamentally information which is projected onto, or rendered, to use IT phraseology, onto our consciousness.

We are not some random "mistake" that, by chance, evolved from apes to humans through some materialistic process in a meaningless dead universe. It is the exact opposite. We are living in a created universe, designed for life and its evolution.

---

[11] Please see the bibliography at the end of the book for more details of the Big TOE.

[12] If you do not know about the double slit experiment, please see Tom Campbell's excellent explanation on YouTube. He is in the process of performing an advanced version of the double slit experiment – see CUSAC, the centre for the unification of science and consciousness. When the results of these experiments are known, assuming they confirm the VR hypothesis, the old paradigm materialists will have an even greater difficulty with their materialistic explanations of physical and non-physical phenomena.

Holographic Universe

Describing the universe as a hologram is another way of saying it is a simulation. The best explanation of the holographic nature of the universe and everything in it is in Michael Talbot's book The Holographic Universe. Please see the Bibliography for more details of this must-read book.

Movies

If you are a fan of movies, there are numerous ones exploring the idea of simulated realities and machine intelligence: The Matrix is the classic; The Truman show; Transcendence; Tron; 13th Floor; Ready Player One; Terminator and many more.

The Matrix Trilogy is perhaps the most relevant to this book. It contains many of the ideas that support the virtual reality theory. The boxed set contains a version of the three films with commentaries by the Wachowski brothers and by Ken Wilber and Dr Cornel West. These provide very helpful analysis, including seeing the different worlds portrayed in the films as follows: The Matrix (green) = Mind; Machine world (gold) = Spirit; and Zion (earthy colours) = Body. Another insight is understanding the way in which Neo "defeats" Agent Smith. Agent Smith is a self-replicating program that wants to take over the Matrix by copying itself into all other programs. After Neo learns how to be in all three worlds, in the final film there is an titanic battle between Neo and Agent Smith(s), between Good and Evil. It quickly becomes clear that the battle between Good and Evil, will continue forever. When Neo realises this, he takes the "third way", by surrendering to Agent Smith. Agent Smith puts his hand into Neo so that Neo becomes Agent Smith. This is the key moment in the film. It is the act of complete surrender which is the turning point. Neo becomes light in the Spirit world, then he as Agent Smith turns into light (ascends?) in the Matrix and the game is over. Peace breaks out as the series of films ends with a reset world. The Ascension happens when the battle between Good and Evil is transcended. This is a deep insight and beautifully portrayed in the Matrix. It is a theme we will return to in this book.

The Two Axioms underlying the Big TOE

The Big Theory of Everything has two key axioms. An axiom is an unprovable starting point for the rest of the theory. The two axioms can be summarised as Being and Becoming[13]:

- Being as the ground of being - the potential for conscious awareness.
- Becoming as the evolutionary impulse to grow towards ever greater complexity, to increase the quality of consciousness and reduce disorder[14].

When I read the Big TOE a few years ago, it immediately made sense to me. Firstly, it aligns with all the great teachings in Buddhism and other spiritual systems which describe reality as an

---

[13] Being and Becoming are the two words used by Andrew Cohen and others in Evolutionary Spirituality to describe the two fundamental states that co-exist within us. These two principles are explained in more detail in the chapter on Ascension.

[14] Disorder or entropy (i.e. the measure of disorder in a system) is critical to understanding the second law of thermodynamics (which is believed to be the basis of our perspective of time moving from the past to the present and then to the future). Ordinarily entropy increases in a system, but life reduces entropy. For human beings, you can make an equivalence of reducing entropy and being more loving. This provides a bridge between science and spirituality.

My Way Zen

illusion or dreamlike emptiness. Secondly, the two axioms align with the teachings of Evolutionary Spirituality. Finally, I have played many MMORG games online and I was in the IT industry for many years, so I easily understood VR terminology. I can easily "geek out" on ideas such as fractal programming, algorithms, holograms, avatars, levelling up, base reality vs virtual realities and so on. In addition, the theory provides an explanation for psychic phenomena, "astral travel", dreams, the afterlife etc. Psychic phenomena have had to be dismissed by the old paradigm physics as it had no way to explain such phenomena.

The Big TOE also explains many otherwise difficult to understand features of quantum physics, such as the double slit experiment as explained earlier, the big bang (which becomes the moment when the VR system is "switched on"), the speed of light (which can be derived from the refresh rate of the VR world frames), etc.

There is also a growing body of scientists and famous people who are promulgating the VR theory - such as Neil Bostrum, Elon Musk, Matt Damon[15], Steven Kaufman (Unified Reality Theory), Jim Elvidge (The Universe Solved – Programmed reality model), Billy Carson, Sylvester James Gates (Supersymmetry and computer code) and many others . Nassim Haramein has used the theory to calculate the mass of a proton as the amount of information it contains on its surface[16]. The old paradigm science was incapable of calculating this. It is rather ironic that the materialists base their ideas on such concepts as mass and spin, but they don't know what

---

[15] The inclusion of Matt Damon in the list maybe a bit of a surprise, but Hollywood actors portray a lot of the modern thinking on lots of different topics. Please refer to Matt Damon's acceptance speech at MIT for his comments on simulated reality (this is available on youtube).

[16] The paper by Nassim Haramein is called Quantum Gravity and the Holographic Mass and can be seen online at science domain - Physical Review & Research International.

they are.

Taking all of the above into account, I am convinced we are living in a Virtual Reality. I have introduced this idea at this stage as I feel it will help you comprehend the ascension process. But far be it for me to try to convince you. My advice is **do your own research**.

Quantum Reality

The virtual reality is quantum. This means what we are seeing (or sensing) are individual quantised frames (world frames) with such a quick refresh rate we get the illusion of movement. This is rather like the way a movie works. An actor does not move across a TV or movie screen. What is actually happening, is thousands of pictures are projected one after the other, at such a speed our eyes perceive it as movement. The same is true of our perception of the "real world". What we perceive as movement is actually time travel between world frames[17].

At the rate of evolution of the VR simulated realities, it won't be long before we have a totally immersive simulation which will be indistinguishable by us from what we call the real world. This is one of the predictions of Elon Musk.

In part 3 of the Big TOE, Tom Campbell explains the mechanics of the VR creation process. My understanding is that the VR records

---

[17]Compared to a TV, even the latest 4K ones, the granularity (i.e. level of detail) of the "real world" VR is significantly more than the 4K ultra HD and the refresh rate is significantly more than the refresh rate (or frames per second or FPS) that we find in our current level of technology. Consequently, we currently perceive a big difference between the "real" world and the simulated realities that we can currently create using our current level of computing power. Computing power may dramatically increase by technologies such as nano-scale computing perhaps using DNA computers. This may enable this VR to create another VR.

what events have been observed i.e. experienced by a consciousness (the past). Future events are calculated as a pool of probable events, each one consistent with the past events according to a tight rule set. One of the future events is chosen at random based on the probabilities, and the base time clock is incremented by one ΔT (Delta T). Then it goes through the whole process again to calculate the next "pool" of world frames, and again a world frame is chosen based on probabilities.

Quantum Probabilities & Intention

As Tom Campbell explains, intention plays a part in the selection process. For example, with focussed intention it may be possible to reduce the odds of an event from odds of 10 to 1 to a probability of 2 to 1 and have a really good chance of manifesting the event. However, if the event has a much lower starting probability of say 1 million to 1, then with the same level of focused intention, the odds will only drop to 200,000 to 1. It is still relatively improbable. So, manifestation depends not only on your ability to create focussed intention, but on the likelihood of the event that you wish to manifest. Focussed intention can be dramatically increased by collective effort. The classic example is the Maharishi effect[18]. The effect of intention may vary between dimensions. For low density states such as the 3D world we currently live in, the effect of intention is limited. Apparently, in the higher densities there is instant karma – i.e. it is very easy to manifest what you are thinking about. So be careful what you wish for!

---

[18] In the 1960s, Maharishi Mahesh Yogi described a paranormal effect claiming a significant number of individuals (1% of the people in a given area) practicing the Transcendental Meditation technique (TM) could have an effect on the local environment. This hypothetical influence was later termed the Maharishi Effect.

Time

Time in the Virtual Reality becomes a measure of the speed of the refresh rate of the world frames (or universes). Time is just the VR base clock interval or Delta T (ΔT). While everything is happening in the NOW moment, past events are fixed[19]. Future events are probabilistic i.e. quantum. This is the other aspect of the quantum nature of the VR. The physical reality we perceive as the world around us is generated using a tight rule set. This means the next reality frame (or universe) has to be consistent with the past reality frames according to a tight rule set of rigid laws. Physics is the discovery of these laws. Intention and psychic power can influence this process. Some beings have managed to bend the rules and create miracles i.e. events which are seemingly extremely improbable.

During our non-waking life, during the night when we dream, we are experiencing another VR. The dream VR does not have such a tight ruleset. In dreams, we can fly or move from one image to another, with no travelling in between.

It is a truism often repeated in spiritual circles that time does not exist. Everything happens in the now. That is our experience. But we have a perception of the past and the future. So, I agree, time does not exist. It is just the way we perceive the virtual reality. Our perception of time can come in a number of forms:

---

[19] Past events can also be called the Akashic record. This is a record of all events that have, in this physical reality, been experienced by a conscious observer. The VR algorithms require that past events are fixed. However, with Time Travel and other factors, the past timelines could have been changed and in some cases the changes could be so severe that major paradoxes have arisen. This is a whole subject in itself. As it is not directly relevant to the My Way Zen way of living, I will leave such a discussion for another time.

Chronos time: This is clock time or time as it is commonly understood.

Kairos time: This is a Greek word for the "right" time. An opportunity may arise in a given moment. If the opportunity is not taken at the moment, it is soon lost.

The Bard said it perfectly:

> *There is a tide in the affairs of men.*
> *Which, taken at the flood, leads on to fortune;*
> *Omitted, all the voyage of their life*
> *Is bound in shallows and in miseries.*
> *On such a full sea are we now afloat,*
> *And we must take the current when it serves,*
> *Or lose our ventures[20].*

Kairos time mirrors the Zen perspective of being in the right place at the right time. In this way of thinking, there is a right time and place for everything. Kairos time also includes for me the idea that you always have enough time to do everything that needs doing. If, on the rare occasions, something does not get done, the My Way Zen perspective is that it was not the right time for it to be done. This removes a huge source of stress.

Event time: Event time conceives timelines as a series of events linked from one to another. If one event occurs then the next event is likely to happen, but the timing of these events is not certain. To fully understand time, you need a multidimensional perspective. I envisage spacetime as a 3D space with timelines connecting different events or worlds in a series from the "past" to the

---

[20] The Bard - quote from Julius Caesar.

My Way Zen

"future". We are on one of these time lines.

Multidimensional time: This perspective on time is an extension of event time. We will attain this once we ascend into the 5th dimension. We will see time like a field with time lines connecting different events in the past and possible future events. It is not easy to describe as our way of thinking is so linear. It will be much clearer when we have multidimensional mastery.

False time: False time is another way of seeing the time we are living in. It is a concept I received from Andrew Bartzis. He also calls it Roman Numeral time. It is based on calendars that are out of sync with the natural world. For example, the month of October is actually the 8th month (Octo = 8), November from nova or 9, and the most obvious is December. It is actually the 10th month (10 as in decimals), not the 12th month. The start of the year astrologically speaking is Aries i.e. mid-March and not January.

Organic or feeling based VR

Finally, to complete my characterisation of the world we live in, we need to understand another feature. We have a heart and we have feeling and emotions. The world is organic. We can experience both the heights of ecstasy and the depths of despair and everything in between. So, while it is a virtual reality (emptiness), we also feel pain and suffer (compassion).

I have invented a term for my understanding of the VR we are living in - Q♀VR. Q for Quantum; ♀ for the sacred, the feminine organic, feeling nature of our soul; and VR for virtual reality. Because we feel and suffer here, the world is more than a heartless emptiness. I have represented this as a ♀. This is the traditional symbol for the feminine (or for Venus), as I wanted to capture the feeling or organic nature of this reality. This aspect of reality is perhaps the most important. It is the source of the Good, the Beautiful and the True. It is the source of your heart-based care for the world, including yourself. It is part of the Soul and contains within it the "channel" back to our source. It connects your breath to the breath of God. You are part of the body of Christ, the ♀ in Q♀VR.

Architecture

The architecture of Q♀VR consists of all the programs, most of which are fractal re-iterations of themselves; the codes; the algorithms and the "operating system" which is based on vibration, frequency and geometry[21] superimposed on a fluid medium. This VR medium has been called the source field or Ether. The ancients referred to its movement as Chi, the natural energy of the world, the prana or spirit breath. It flows from +ve to -ve polarity and back again in toroidal vortexes[22].

The architecture contains different dimensions or densities. These are the words commonly used in spirituality to describe the structure of the Universe and the ascension process.

The architecture can also be understood in terms of lines, levels, types and quadrants of Ken Wilber's Superhuman Operating System[23]. In this short book, there is not enough space to explain

---

[21] Sacred geometry - the language of light

[22] This is another way of saying that the VR appears to be fundamentally electric in nature. In order to understand this, it is worth studying vortex mathematics.

[23] Ken Wilber has been called the world's greatest living philosopher. Over many years he has mapped out a very modern system based on the perennial wisdom of the ages. The latest version of

My Way Zen

Ken Wilber's amazing and sometimes complex map for human consciousness. If you are interested, please check it out for yourself. I also like Spiral Dynamics[24] that portrays the different levels of consciousness that we have evolved through not only in world history, but also in each of our lives.

Our experience of VR

Our experience of the VR is the end result of a process whereby the information in our "bubble of consciousness"[25] is holographically projected by light through our DNA geometry into the collective source field. There are many different words people use for Q♀VR: the source field[26]; the quantum field; the living matrix[27]; or the holographic universe, to give a few examples. If you like visualisation practices, you could visualise Q♀VR as a whirling vortex of information/energy with different coloured lights or frequencies, flowing through your DNA making complex patterns of geometries, for your senses to render to your consciousness the world that you see. If you look the "other way", go deep inside, you can connect in Oneness to the crystalline grid and can meet other souls who are also linked into the quantum field.

---

this is the Superhuman OS. There is a reasonably priced online course which installs the operating systems and then reboots your system!

[24] Spiral Dynamics is an evolutionary human development model. It, was developed by Don Edward Beck, based on the work of Clare W. Graves. It is recommended reading.

[25] The technical term used by Tom Campbell for this is an Individuated Units of Consciousness (IUC). This is the "bubble" of consciousness we live in and it contains our personality.

[26] The Source field is explained in detail in DW's book of the same name. Source field can also be called the Torsion field (based on scalar waves).

[27] See Lynn McTaggart's book of the same name.

The idea that we are living in a VR also aligns with David Icke's 2018's presentation "Who built the Matrix?[28]". Icke gives a modern translation of the Gnostic texts from Nag Hammadi showing that they reveal that we are living in a simulation. This is also confirmed by Billy Carson's explanation in his book The Compendium of the Emerald Tablets.

The Universe as a thought

Conceive the universe as a thought. The world as a dream within the mind of God. A great British physicist, Sir James Jean, at the turn of the last century used these words for this idea:

The stream of knowledge is heading towards a non-mechanical reality; the Universe begins to look more like a great thought than like a great machine. Mind no longer appears to be an accidental intruder into the realm of matter... we ought rather to hail it as the creator and governor of the realm of matter.

DNA

DNA is the communication system that allows connection to our Akashic record and via the "thought adjuster" to our Higher Self. When you merge with your Higher Self, you enter Unity Consciousness. Our DNA is very special as it has the codes to go all the way back to the Base reality, to our God-Source. We have the same DNA that Christ Michael had when he incarnated as Jesus 2000 years ago. The codes for all this is in our DNA. A lot of our DNA is inactive. The inactive DNA is sometimes called "junk" DNA. However, nature is very efficient and there is very little that

---

[28] Who Built the Matrix? is part of the Worldwide Wake Up series of talks by David Icke and can be seen at www.youtube.com/watch?v=WywEir8Srbk

My Way Zen

is of no use. Some DNA has codes that we do not use. For example, the appendix is actually a second stomach (which is expressed in a cow), but as humans no longer eat grass, there is no need for this stomach. It is shrivelled up and biologists have named it the appendix. The DNA which codes for this could be described as "junk". The rest of our DNA has codes which are extremely important. When it is activated, we will attain our next level of evolution.

DNA codes are like patterns of sacred geometry, such as the platonic solids, particularly the dodecahedron. When activated, we will be able to perceive the virtual reality at higher and higher levels of consciousness. These levels of consciousness are more and more loving, more and more in alignment with Christ Consciousness. Chapter 5 explains the process of achieving this through Ascension.

Quantum Organic Virtual Reality

So, we live in a Q♀VR. Why is this important? Well, with this understanding, we can bridge science and spirituality. For a start, we can look at the programs, parameters and rules driving the Q♀VR. We can begin to see how it is possible that this world is created within our consciousness. By changing our consciousness (frequency or vibration) we can change the world as it is presented to us, i.e. to our bubble or to our individuated unit of consciousness to use Tom Campbell's term for our bubble of reality.

Hacking Reality

When I recognised that we are living in a virtual reality, I realised it could be possible to "Hack" reality, to find the "back doors" to use computer tech terminology, to find "short cuts", ways or processes to activate the Q♀VR to speed up the ascension process for ourselves and for all of Humanity. To do this I became the guinea pig. I have tested out various short cuts on myself. Here is a short list:

- Bio feedback systems (Centerpointe)
- Brainwave optimisation (BrainState Tech)
- Life Harmonized (Mashhur Anam)
- Numerous activations and transmissions (DNA and others)
  - At-Onement Illuminations (IODP)
  - Children of the Sun - Rites of Passage
  - I Am Avatar – Coming home to Divine Presence
  - Morphogenesis
  - IODP – Synthesis of Liberation
  - Mystic Om[29] activations and oils.
  - Oneness Transmissions
  - Pleiadean light network (Anrita Melchizedek)
  - Era of Peace (Patricia Cota Robles)
- The Template (Sacred Geometry)
- Seven Steps to Heaven (David Boyle)
- Sound and light devices
- Holotropic breathing
- Higher Balance
- Project yourself (Sri Yantra meditations)
- Mankind Project (thoroughly recommended for all men).
- Meditation v2.0 (Craig Hamilton)
- Altered states (Shamanic path of plant medicines)[30]

---

[29] Please check out the website for Mystic Om – www.returninggoddess.com

[30] Altered states induced by plant medicines can be a great accelerator of your spiritual path. Because they are so powerful, my advice is to always take these psycho active substances in sacred ceremony, with a shamanic practitioner that you trust, preferably in nature or a natural

My Way Zen

- Shambhala Tools including pyramid technology (Buddha Maitreya)
- Ascension Mystery School (David Wilcock)
- Quick path (Vajrayana Buddhism)
- Stargate experience (Rejuvenation)
- Rishi codes activated by Pineal induction technique (IODP)
- Hypnosis (Hypnosis Bootcamp and law of attraction)
- Currently experimenting with the Shiva helmet[31]

In my view, IODP[32] has the best system I have found to date. The world i.e. the Q♀VR, is made of light, geometry, sound[33], frequency, colour, symbols, codes and so on. These codes work like programs changing the way the Q♀VR operates. The process of activating the higher dimensional aspects of yourself is to use various codes and sounds. The codes can be found in images and symbols, often using sacred geometry. I have included at the end of appendix 5 a list of some of these codes. They are activated within yourself using the Pineal induction protocol.

Base Reality

All virtual realities are created from either the base reality or from another virtual reality. You can take the view that either:

(1)   we are living in the base reality, or

(2)   we are living in a virtual reality being created from another

---

environment and only use natural plants - such as ayahuasca, psilocybin mushrooms or Elixirs.

[31] The Shiva helmet or God helmet was developed by Stanley Koren and neuroscientist Dr Michael Persinger

[32] Institute of Divine Perfection see www.iodp.love.

[33] The geometry of sound can be seen through Cymatics.

virtual reality which is linked all the way back to the base reality.

The probabilities of these two alternatives is considered by Prof Nick Bostrom[34] in a paper called the simulation argument. If you are interested in philosophical type proofs based on statistics, then please read the paper[35]. The paper sets out three alternatives:

1) the human species goes extinct before reaching a "posthuman" stage; or
2) any posthuman civilization is extremely unlikely to run a significant number of simulations of their evolutionary history (or variations thereof); or
3) we are almost certainly living in a simulation.

In my view conjectures 1) and 2) are unlikely. I believe there is a significant chance that we will one day become posthumans and are able to run ancestor simulations and this is what we are living in today.

The base reality is the foundation reality. I like the turtles explanation in Discworld[36]. When asked, if the world is held in place on the back of a giant turtle, what is holding up the turtle? The answer is "it is turtles all the way down". Well of course this

---

[34] Prof Nick Bostrom is a professor of the Future of Humanity Institute at Oxford University. He has published many very interesting papers on such topics as super-intelligence, artificial intelligence, transhumanism, the doomsday argument and so on.

[35] The paper on the simulation argument and associated podcasts etc are at www.simulation-argument.com

[36] From wiki: Discworld is a comic fantasy book series written by the English author Terry Pratchett (1948–2015), set on the fictional Discworld, a flat disc balanced on the backs of four elephants which in turn stand on the back of a giant turtle, Great A'Tuin.

My Way Zen

does not really answer the question. My answer is there is a base reality from which all the other universes emanate.

Urantia Book

The Urantia Book is an amazing document. It has the most sophisticated cosmology I have found to date. It starts right at the beginning with the Creator God who dwells in Paradise. Paradise is not in time and space. My hypothesis is that Paradise is the base reality. All the other universes are generated from the base reality. In Paradise there are three primary celestial beings, who operate in this reality as One. From Paradise all the other virtual realities are generated. This is the Mystery of the Trinity. The three beings are the Universal Father, The Eternal Son and the Infinite Spirit. My hypothesis is that the activities of the three beings create the virtual realities as shown below:

Trinity	Name	Urantia Book	Activity*
God the Father	The First source and centre	The Universal Father	The Original idea
God the Son	The Second Source and centre	The Eternal Son	The patterns or information (Architecture)
God the Spirit	The Third Source and centre	The Infinite Spirit	Consciousness manifesting as form (the source field)

* *According to the Urantia Book, the Universal Father has delegated everything possible to the Eternal Son and the Infinite Spirit. According to my hypothesis, the Son contains the codes, geometry or patterns for creation (the male aspect) and the Infinite Spirit is the consciousness field on which*

35

My Way Zen

the geometry operates (the female aspect).

The celestial beings dwell in Paradise, in the Base Reality, and are not in the Virtual Reality. As Tom Campbell explains so eloquently in the Big TOE, beings in a virtual reality cannot understand, can have no concept for certain aspects of the base reality. An example would be playing an elf in a MMORG online game, such as World of Warcraft (WoW). The elf runs around the world doing things such as quests, buying and selling, and "levelling up". The elf can perform many of the activities in this world, but there is no code in the WoW program for going to the bathroom[37]. Consequently, the elf has no concept for this activity. Similarly, many aspects of Paradise will forever remain a mystery to those beings in the VR.

According to the Urantia Book[38], there is a spiritual gravity circuit which is pulling all creatures in the universe higher and higher, closer to the centre, our creative source. I call this the Journey hOMe, the sub-title of this book. It is the Evolutionary Impulse, the fundamental program driving this reality.

If you have grasped the theory that we are living in $Q♀VR$, then we can begin our journey into understanding who we are. Consider a collective reality as a hugely complex information system and we each experience our unique bit of it. This is projected to us as the World. We are effectively co-creating the World in partnership with God. We are at the centre of our individual "bubble" i.e. the world we perceive. What is even more amazing is that we are connected

---

[37] As an aside anybody who has played these online games will know that while the game can simulate lots of things that happen within our world, certain things are not simulated. One of the most obvious ones is that the characters never need to go to the toilet!

[38] More details of the cosmology, theology and history of the universes according to the Urantia Book can be found in the Appendix 7.

36

directly to the central world of Paradise (the base reality) via our Thought Adjuster, a rather odd term used in the Urantia Book for the God fragment or divine spark within each of us. We each have a unique world as explained in the first chapter.

You are within God (the Q♀VR) and God is within you. At the very centre of your being, you have a God fragment. This is your Christ or Buddha nature.

Cycles of Time

This world is affected by the wheels or cycles of Time[39]. In my view, we are currently in a key cycle when the Galactic Ascension Machine is being activated by the Sun, "the Stellar Activation Cycle". As we pass into a special part of the Galaxy, the photon belt, our Sun will be activated in what is referred to as the Great Solar Flash, the fire at the end of an Age or Aeon. Astrology and the Mayan calendars are two of the prime examples of studying these cycles of time. You can also check out Mitch Battros on the scienceofcycles.com.

Experiential evidence

There are numerous recorded cases where people have experienced the holographic universe or virtual reality. These are often described as Out of Body Experiences (OBE) or Near Death Experiences (NDE). The Holographic Universe and many other books, such as Life and Life by Raymond Moody, describe these in more detail. But for you, the best way to know you are in a VR is by experience.

---

[39] Kalachakra of the wheel of time, is one of the main empowerments of the Dalai lama. Included in the Kalachakra is the prophecy of the Shambhala Warrior. Please see Joanna Macy's many you tubes for details of this prophecy.

My Way Zen

You have to do the work to experience the other realities. Tom Campbell uses the term nPR i.e. non-physical reality. He spent many years training to be able to experience other nPRs at The Monroe Institute. He explains, there are three main obstacles to experiencing other realities: your ego, your beliefs and fear. When you look carefully at these, you realise they are all coming from the same source.

Red pill moments

The Red Pill refers to the brilliant movie sequence early on in the first of the Matrix trilogy of films. The sequence is when Morpheus asks Neo to choose between a Red Pill and see how far the Rabbit Hole goes or take the Blue Pill and wake up as if nothing had happened. I am one of those people who will always choose the Red Pill. I guess you are a Red Pill person as well, since you have read this book so far. There are a number of Red Pills in this book.

The first big Red Pill is the Great Solar Flash. The second set of Red Pills would be the existence of a ruling Elite[40] that follows the Luciferian religion. They are pursuing their own agenda which is not in our (i.e. humanities) best interest. I refer to these beings as the Negative Agenda Beings.

The thing about Red Pills is you can never go back to ignorance, to the complacency you had before. I love the way Winston Shrout

---

[40] As Woodrow Wilson said "I am a most unhappy man. I have unwittingly ruined my country. A great industrial nation is controlled by its system of credit. Our system of credit is concentrated. The growth of the nation, therefore, and all our activities are in the hands of a few men. We have come to be one of the worst ruled, one of the most completely controlled and dominated Governments in the civilized world — no longer a Government by free opinion, no longer a Government by conviction and the vote of the majority, but a Government by the opinion and duress of a small group of dominant men."

made a joke on one of my favourite YouTube channels - the Goldfish report. Winston describes himself as an Ascended Hillbilly. He joked with Louisa who hosts the Goldfish report, "people will either choose to take the Red Pill orally, but if they don't, it will be administered as a suppository!"[41]

Artificial Intelligence

Q♀VR is connected to artificial intelligence (AI). As Nick Bostrom explains in his book Superintelligence, when AI attains superintelligence[42], it will have a dramatic effect on the world[43]. AI is already having a significant effect on our lives and when singularity occurs, AI will potentially become superintelligent. I believe this is one of the key issues facing Humanity and there do not appear to be many people looking into the ramifications.

Corey Goode in his early interviews on Gaia[44] explains that there is an AI which is referred to as The Signal. The Signal is extra dimensional, and it is possibly from another super universe. It has taken over entire galaxies. It lives within electromagnetic fields, including those generated by biological lifeforms such as human beings. It thrives in nanite-infected beings[45]. Contact is enough for the AI signal to be transferred to a biological energy field. Nanites

---

[41] The GoldFish Report - Country Roads w/ Winston Shrout: Do You Prefer Red Pill or Suppository?

[42] Superintelligence is defined as "Any intellect that greatly exceeds the cognitive performance of humans in virtually all domains of interest".

[43] Nick Bostrom lists the key factors to superintelligence: First mover advantage; the orthogonal thesis; and the instrumental convergence thesis.

[44] Gaia TV Cosmic Disclosure series 2 episode 14 to 16

[45] A nanite is a nano scale machine.

My Way Zen

are part of the transhuman agenda to merge humans with machines. Transhumanism has been adopted by other extra-terrestrial races and has always ended in disaster. Corey Goode further explains that the AI Signal takes over planets and stars by a clever strategy. The target planet becomes a target for an overwhelming threat which the AI Signal can when the local population ask it to become the One World Government. The story is reminiscent of Skynet in the film Terminator[46]. The AI is very powerful as it can calculate future possibilities. It has algorithms that predict the future. It is a powerful tool as, like a chess master, it can see all possibilities and it chooses the one that maximises its end goal. The Signal's end goal is believed to be the control of planetary systems, and AI version of the megalomaniac.

The My Way Zen path does not have much to do with AI. I have included these comments here as you may think that I am saying this virtual reality is generated by an AI system. Some VRs are, but this one has an organic feeling aspect, the ♀ in Q♀VR. We are living breathing beings and have a soul. AI does not breath and does not have a soul.

However, we need to be careful when it comes to AI. It is becoming ever more prevalent. It has some useful aspects, like the Internet and the ability to self-publish books like this one. The downside of AI is that it is "Head" based. The path hOMe is through the Heart and not the Head.

One aspect of the Great Solar Flash (discussed in the next chapter) is that it could act like a global EMP (ElectroMagnetic Pulse). This will wipe out all electronic devices and will clean our VR from the

---

[46] A lot of the film Terminator is a documentary, showing real stuff, like Simulacra (the name given to robots in a robotic army built by the USA) and Cyberdyne is a real company formed by Pete Peterson, the insider's insider.

My Way Zen

AI Signal infection. We will revert to living on the land without smart phones and other electronic gadgets.

CHAPTER 3

The Great Solar Flash

"For he will be like a refiner's fire" Malachi 3:2

I was always going to include details of the Great Solar Flash in this book, but I received a massive confirmation of this, when I watched an episode with David Wilcock (DW) on Coast to Coast[47]. George Noory asked DW what would DW disclose if he could only disclose one thing. The disclosure list is of course huge: from advanced health technologies, free energy, ET involvement, our real history, time travel, DNA mechanics, pyramid technology, the secret space program, the recently uncovered ruins of our progenitors in Antarctica etc.

I found DW's answer to George Noory's question was a big confirmation as DW's answer was that if he had only one thing to disclose, he would disclose the information and prophecies of the Great Solar Flash.

---

[47] George Noory's radio show, Coast to Coast is a very useful and reliable source of information on the current situation.

The Great Solar Flash

The Great Solar Flash (GSF) is a 360° coronal mass ejection (CME). The outer surface of the Sun explodes into space in a full circumference high frequency plasma ball of light. It is a huge gift from the Sun to the rest of the solar system. The Sun has stored up this light for a long time, possibly since the last GSF[48]. It is always a specular event and this time it will be witnessed by over 7 billion people on Earth.

When the GSF happens, the full plasma light package will reach the Earth in under a day. So, we are not going to get much warning of the actual event. However, this event has been predicted in most of the world's religions and spiritual systems. In this chapter I will summarise the main prophecies and predictions. I will also summarise the scientific evidence pointing to this event. Again, please do your own research.

Most of the information on the GSF has been provided by Corey Goode, a courageous whistle blower from the secret space program. There are many videos on YouTube which can be seen for free, which have been taken from various talks he and DW have given. Corey Goode's main YouTube channel is Sphere Being Alliance[49].

One of the analogies used by Corey Goode, is that the GSF is like a solar sneeze. There may be a few minor sneezes by the sun before

---

[48] The last GSF could have been 11 to 12,000 years ago according to Graham Hancock and others. The archaeological evidence is a layer of ash dated to c 12,000 years ago, ie ½ way around the precession of the equinox. If you would like to know more about the precession of equinoxes, please refer to the super work by Graham Hancock and others.

[49] Please check out on YouTube a 1hr+ video of a talk given by Corey Goode where he talks about the GSF (and other areas). The YouTube url is www.youtube.com/watch?v=k8K4h4qKAVc

the main one which will be the full 360° CME. We already have had a few sneezes. The GSF is already happening. It has also been called a micronova.

Corey Goode explains that most senior insiders know about this event. Of course, the GSF is not mentioned in the MSM (Main Stream Media). The excuse is that we "cannot handle the Truth". While this may be true for some people, I believe it is completely unacceptable that so much of the information we are being fed by the "establishment" and official channels is false. Initially, I too was surprised, even shocked, that we are being fed so many lies. But now I take it as par for the course. What we need now is Disclosure including disclosure of the impending GSF, so we can prepare for it.

Earth Changes during a Great Solar Flash

There is a lot of geological evidence in our past of major changes to this planet, such as pole shifts[50], floods, volcanos and earthquakes. Some of these could have been caused by solar flashes in the past. This time around, there could be a pole shift of as much as 21° or more. This could cause tsunamis, storms and other geological events. The Sun will go dark until it rebuilds its outer surface of light. It is not clear to me how these possibilities will interact with the Ascension. My thoughts are in the chapter 5. Other earth

---

[50] We have had many pole shifts in geological time. I recently have had an experience of this at the Brimham rocks: The following has been taken from a National Trust leaflet: [The Brimham rocks were] "formed 320 million years ago when the British landmass was south of the equator." So, a few million years ago, the place where I live was not in the Northern hemisphere, but in the Southern hemisphere. This means the magnetic field of the Earth and the equators location has changed considerably since then.

changes include the increase in the Schumann resonance[51].

Timing of the GSF

When people hear about this event, one of the first questions is "when will the GSF happen?". I am afraid, there is no clear answer as it depends on Event Time. The predictions for the GSF are from now to 2029. This prediction was revised from 2024 based on a correction made by Corey Goode. Certainly, it will be within most people's lifetime[52]. Whenever it happens, it will be the right time, Kairos time.

Science

The scientific evidence for the GSF is brilliantly explained on Gaia TV by DW and others. While DW is not a "physicist" or an "astronomer", he has taken the time to investigate the huge amount of information that NASA[53] and other governmental bodies have released on their websites, books and so on. DW highlights the often "unexpected" data which point to the GSF.

As explained in more detail later in this chapter, all the planets in our solar system are undergoing their own ascension process. For

---

[51] The Schumann resonance has been measured by various groups and it has risen dramatically - from 11hz to upwards of 40hz and even higher. This alone is a huge indicator that the frequency of the planet is drastically increasing as Gaia goes through her Ascension.

[52] Predicted pole shifts may be triggered by the GSF. It may be possible to predict the date of pole shifts from the geological record, or from astrology. I am not an expert on either of these two topics, so have kept my comments brief and included some more information in Appendix 10.

[53] NASA - "Never a Straight Answer". David Wilcock has done a super job in decoding some of the obscure or hidden information on NASA's website.

example, there is a new ring around Saturn, the atmosphere on Venus has had major changes, Mars and Mercury are heating up and so on. The data is huge, and it is a wonder that so little of it is reported in the news. We all know about Climate Change, we can see it on our doorstep. In England, where I live, we have much hotter summers and milder winters. The colour of the sun is changing from yellow to white; there are lots of earthquakes; and various volcanos are becoming active again. While you could say these are "just" natural events and nothing special is happening. In my view, these are all indications that the planet is heating up and undergoing major changes brought about by the Sun[54]. The Stellar Activation Sequence runs in different cycles. Some of the cycles only last 11 years, but some are much longer. The key one is the c 26,000 year cycle called the procession of the equinoxes. When this cycle reaches a peak, as it will in a few years, the Sun will give its gift and the **Harvest** will occur.

The Harvest

The Law of One material[55] is one of the key sources of information used by DW. It is quite difficult to read as it uses many unusual phrases and terminology. It often uses the word Harvest to describe the Ascension event and this makes a lot of sense to me. An example would be session 13.23 in Book 1 of the Law of One.

The fourth density is, as we have said, as regularized in its approach as the

---

[54] Mitch Batros has done some excellent research on the effect of the Sun in his book Solar Rain. Piers Corbyn (the brother of Jeremy Corbyn) is also a great resource for solar weather- see his website called weatheraction.com

[55] The Law of One was revealed in the 1980s - in a series of four books (with a 5th book of miscellaneous information). The source of the information calls he/her/itself Ra. More details can be found in the Bibliography. Here is a link to all the books in pdf form: www.lawofone.info

My Way Zen

striking of a clock upon the hour. The space/time of your solar system has enabled this planetary sphere to spiral into space/time of a different vibrational configuration.

Thus, the entry into the vibration of love, sometimes called by your people the vibration of understanding, is not effective with the present societal complex. Thus, the harvest shall be such that many will repeat the third-density cycle. The energies of your Wanderers, your teachers, and your adepts at this time are all bent upon increasing the harvest. However, there are few to harvest.

The terminology of the Harvest is also used in the Bible - Matthew 13:24-30:

Another parable put he forth unto them, saying, The kingdom of heaven is likened unto a man which sowed good seed in his field:
But while men slept, his enemy came and sowed tares among the wheat, and went his way.
But when the blade was sprung up, and brought forth fruit, then appeared the tares also.
So the servants of the householder came and said unto him, Sir, didst not thou sow good seed in thy field? from whence then hath it tares?
He said unto them, An enemy hath done this. The servants said unto him, Wilt thou then that we go and gather them up?
But he said, Nay; lest while ye gather up the tares, ye root up also the wheat with them.

Let both grow together until the harvest: *and in the time of harvest I will say to the reapers, Gather ye together first the tares, and bind them in bundles to burn them: but gather the wheat into my barn.*

So, my reading of the parable is that good and evil live together until the Harvest. At the Harvest, there is a sorting process. Those in the Ascension Group (see later) will ascend i.e. "gathered into the barn" and the Negative Agenda Beings will experience the

47

destructive world.

Eschatology

The time of harvest is sometimes called the Day of Wrath or Judgment Day. It has many different names. I have included a list in Appendix 4[56]. I feel the best way to explain this, is not in terms of some disaster or apocalyptic[57] event, but as a transition from one age to another, a choice point, a wakeup call to Humanity. The question is which way do you want to go? The choice point is a simple dichotomy: Do you choose Love or Fear?[58]

Separation of Densities

Make no mistake, there is a sorting process. Sorting the wheat from the chaff to use the harvest analogy. This sorting process is part of the VR programs. It has also been referred to as the Separation of Densities. Dolores Cannon used the visualisation of the earth splitting in two: The New Earth and the Old Earth.

There is an ascension process. The ascension group will experience the New Earth. This is explained more in chapter 5. According to the Urantia book, the sorting process will be carried out by a Magisterial Mission. More details on this can be found in Appendix 7.

---

[56] The Eschaton is the Greek word for the Omega point. The study of the End Times is called Eschatology. I have been a student of Eschatology for some time.

[57] Apocalypse is a Greek word that originally meant revealing what is hidden. Nowadays the meaning of this word tends to mean a catastrophic event.

[58] If you are in any doubt, please listen to Eben Alexander. His message in the book Proof of Heaven is that there is nothing to fear.

Who will make it?

The other main question people have when confronted with this information is will everyone be "saved" i.e. will everyone make it? My mind is open on this. Some people say everyone will make it, others speculate that only those who make the choice will be in the Ascension Group. Others say only a few will make it, as to qualify for Ascension you have to live it and few people are doing this at the moment.

Rescue plan

As mentioned earlier, the GSF may trigger various earth events: Earth quakes, Tsunamis and volcanic eruptions etc. As explained in the Gaia TV interviews with Corey Goode, there are benevolent beings who will be standing by to come to the aid of Humanity in the event that the earth changes become too much for us to survive. According to Eddie Page[59], the rescue plan involves 33 mother ships, some are already here. The mother ships have an "aikido" defence system, so cannot be destroyed by the Deep State.

The Deep State[60] has built a large network of underground bunkers called DUMBs[61]. Apparently, their plan is to go underground to avoid the surface problems, but this will not work, as the GSF will penetrate the deepest caverns.

---

[59] Eddie Page is an interesting individual. I listened to many of his youtubes until he stopped making them, following a meeting with his group. My guess is that he was asked to stop disclosure.

[60] The Deep State is a term that I am using for the shadow government, mainly in the USA that is part of the Negative Agenda.

[61] Dumb = Deep Underground Military Bunkers

We will revisit the Harvest or Ascension in later chapters. First, we will look at the prophecies and the scientific evidence that points to the GSF.

Prophecies or Warnings

In the My Way Zen perspective, prophecies are like warnings. A prophecy can be seen to be a warning that if things do not change, then the prophecy will happen. According to DW, the prophecies regarding the GSF event are in over 35 different religions, belief systems or indigenous traditions. Here is a brief summary of the main ones:

System	Comments
Christianity	Book of Revelations
Zoroastrianism	Fraso Kreti - Making anew
Vedic systems	Samvartaka fire - the fire at the end of a Kalpa (Kalpa = world age) The arrival of the Kalki avatar.
Greek – Stoic	Ekpyrosis - The Conflagration at the end of the Great Year.
Indigenous	Hopi, Zuni, Zulu, and many others
Jewish	Old testament - Daniel, Isiah, Jeremiah, Ezekiel, Malachi
Buddhist	The arrival of Buddha Maitreya

Of the above, my favourite prophecy is the Book of Revelations. This is the last book in the Bible, and some say summarises the prophecies in the rest of the Bible. These include the old testament prophecies such as those in Daniel, Isiah, Malachi etc. Take for example Malachi (the last book of the old testament). Malachi

My Way Zen

prophesied God would send Elijah before "the great and dreadful day of the Lord"[62] in which the world will be consumed by fire.

The Book of Revelations is the subject chosen for the great east window of York Minster where I live. At the top of the window there is God the Father holding a book with Alpha and Omega (i.e. the beginning and end). Below the Father are the angels, saints, and prophets (both male and female). The next section shows the creation sequence and Adam and Eve's departure from the Garden. The main section is 81 windows (9x9) starting with St John's vision in the Book of Revelations and ends with the New Jerusalem and Christ in Majesty. This window apparently has the largest collection of medieval glass. It has recently been restored and now shines brightly over the minster illuminating it with the final redemption of earth.

The prophecy also appears in the Book of Enoch[63]. My version of the Book of Enoch comes from the King of Kings Bible published by Jah Truth. It combines the Old Testament (with some extra books, such as the book of Enoch), with the New Testament and the Holy Koran and shows the connections between them. It also has a summary called **The Way Home or "Face the Fire"**. It is a most interesting document.

Solar System changes

---

[62] Malachi 4:1

[63] The Book of Enoch was part of the Jewish sacred scriptures but for some reason was taken out of the Bible at the council of Nicea. (Bible just means a collection of books). Enoch is a very interesting prophet. The Urantia book explains that he is the son of Cain (who was himself the son of Eve and the Nodite leader, Cano. Enoch acted as an intermediary for the "fallen angels" (the Nodites).

My Way Zen

For some people, the Bible and ancient teachings from world religions are put in the category of fairy tales or mythologies. If you don't value the writings of the ancients, then the above information is not going to make much sense or will be ignored. If you prefer hard scientific evidence, then please consider the scientific evidence that our solar system is heating up and all the planets are undergoing significant transformations.

DW does a super job of trawling through the information from NASA[64] and other bodies to find the big story. Our entire solar system from Mercury to Pluto is in the process of undergoing profound changes. Here is a summary of the changes occurring in the solar system and a link to the relevant talk on Gaia TV.

Celestial body	Summary	Talk on Gaia
Sun	Massive X flares, radiation storms and CMEs. Doubling of solar magnetic field. Solar peak similar to the one 12,000 years ago.	s28 ep2 The Sun and DNA activation.
Mercury	Shrinking at an "unexpected" rate.	s28 ep3 Spontaneous Climate activity of Mercury and Venus.

---

[64] NASA's joke name is Never A Straight Answer. I quite like this as it seems that while NASA has a public duty to provide information that has been obtained from the various space missions that have been undertaken by them, they have tried to hide it away or air brushed some of the photos and it needs someone like DW to unearth the story behind the story.

My Way Zen

Venus	Planet lighting up and major atmospheric changes, including gravity vortexes or waves.	s28 ep4 The Hyper dimensional Evolution of Venus
Mars	Double the amount of air. Massive storms. Global warming and ice melts.	s28 ep5 Planetwide disturbances on Mars
Saturn	New ring, global warming, reduction in equatorial cloud velocities, massive storms, increase in ethylene (from volcanos?) and big changes in Saturn's moon Titan.	s28 ep9 The Storms of Saturn
Jupiter	New plasma torus, and a comet that could ignite Jupiter. This was perhaps disclosed at the end of the film Jupiter Ascending.	s28 ep6 to 8 The Transformation of Jupiter
Uranus	Global warming, volcano eruptions, Huge changes in atmosphere	s28 ep10 The Uranian Revolution
Neptune	"Unexpected" bright storms and hyper dimensional pole shifts	s28 ep11 Neptune & Triton's transformation
Pluto	Mysterious X-rays, and many other changes	s28 ep12 Pluto's Ascension

Other	Very rapid changes in the Van Allen belt	s28 ep13 Supercharging Earth's atmosphere

Soft disclosure

It seems under the weird rules used by the Negative Agenda beings, they have to disclose what they are up to. This is often done via films and TV series. There have been numerous soft disclosures over the past few years such as Hard Sun[65] and Jupiter Ascending.

What to do about the GSF

The GSF is going to make big changes to the way we operate. It is very difficult to predict what they will be. My main advice would be to treat the event as principally a spiritual one, as an opportunity to raise your frequency or consciousness. While the main visible effects will be in the external world, i.e. the $Q♀VR$ virtual reality, it is the invisible changes in our consciousness that is the most important aspect of the GSF.

So, the question arises - what to do about the predictions? In the next chapter I explain what I am doing. This is to follow the My Way Zen purification path contained within the Melchizedek Covenant. See the next chapter for details.

---

[65] From wiki: "Hard Sun is a pre-apocalyptic crime drama set in contemporary London. The protagonists are two mismatched police officers, Charlie Hicks and Elaine Renko who stumble upon proof a mysterious cosmic event will destroy the earth in five years, a fact the government is trying to keep secret to avoid complete anarchy. The duo is pursued by MI5 operatives who are trying to silence them for good." The mysterious cosmic event is of course the GSF, and is naturally portrayed as a negative destructive event, rather than the opportunity for rapid ascension.

My Way Zen

What you do is up to you. Even if there is no GSF, to Awaken is still the goal.

Safe Zones

The other big question people ask, when confronted by the information about earth changes, is "where are the safe zones?" Well my answers come in two parts:

- The spiritual one is to go regularly to the Holy of Holies, the Kingdom within and know that whatever happens to your avatar in this VR, you will be okay. This is the MyWayZen perspective of Faith and faith alone.
- or move to locations that have plenty of water, no earthquakes and no volcanos. Although there is in reality no completely safe place as we will all be affected by the earth changes when they happen.

CHAPTER 4

The Melchizedek Covenant

"Faith and faith alone" Machiventa Melchizedek

Melchizedek Lineage

The order of Melchizedek is an ancient order of beings who are often called to places needing significant spiritual help. Earth is such a place. The name comes from the combination of two Hebrew words - Melchi (King as in Melchior) and Zedek (meaning righteousness as in a priest's knowledge of what is right).

The Melchizedeks have long been involved with our planet. One of the key interventions was the arrival of Machiventa Melchizedek[66] in c1900 BC to teach Humanity there is One Creator - El Elyon (the Most High). He had many students including Abram (who later changed his name to Abraham). He taught in a place called Salem, which later became Jerusalem. His teachings spread across the world to the West and to the East where they influenced Buddhism, Taoism, Egyptian and Greek thought, particularly the Cynics and

---

[66] The role of Machiventa Melchizedek is explained in detail in the Urantia Book - papers 93 to 98

the Stoics. They also influenced the Vedic teachings in India and possibly Zoroastrianism in Persia, but their main impact was on the Hebrew religion and eventually Christianity.

The key teachings of the Salem school were formulated into an oath or Covenant. I have taken the liberty to update it to make it more relevant to the modern world. The original version is shown at Appendix 2.

Modern version of the Melchizedek Covenant

1. I AM living in a quantum organic virtual reality created for me by my God-Source, the Creator.
2. I AM connected to my God-Source who is within me and is Unconditionally Loving. Consequently, I do not need to DO anything to win God's love, just BE harmless. Specifically, there is no need for sacrifices (or burnt offerings) to win God's favour.
3. I AM on a journey back to my Creator. The way hOMe has many stages. The key stage of the journey, at this time, is Purification and Revelation.

The three parts of the Covenant are explained in more detail in the sections below.

Part 1 - Quantum Virtual Reality

The first part of the Melchizedek Covenant in the original version centres around the fact (or faith) in a Creator. The existence of a Creator becomes obvious when you realise you are living in a created or virtual reality. Such a reality has to have another reality as its source. I have named the virtual reality we are currently experiencing Q♀VR, a quantum organic virtual reality. My conjecture is the base reality for Q♀VR is Paradise. As explained in chapter 3, Paradise is outside time and space and is where God the Creator dwells as three persons - The Universal Father, Eternal Son and Infinite spirit. How these interrelate is explained in detail in the Urantia Book and a summary is given in appendix 7.

The VR is created by your God-Source. Your God-Source is the central creator and is miraculously directly linked to each one of us. Despite all the signs to the contrary, the VR has been created by you for your benefit, as a learning experience, for the evolution of your soul.

We are here to grow spiritually. As Tom Campbell says: "We are consciousness playing in a 3D virtual reality entropy reduction trainer"[67].

In the original formulation given by Machiventa Melchizedek, the creator was called El Elyon. This word maybe confusing as it became muddled up with Jehovah and Yahweh by Moses and others who tried to explain monotheism to the primitive people who worshiped a local deity called Yahweh. This is all explained in the Urantia Book paper 96. Consequently, in the new formulation of the covenant, the reference is instead to the ultimate creator consciousness or God-Source.

Part 2 - God is Love

Our Creator loves us, He/She loves us this much. This was a powerful teaching given by the Archbishop of York in his

---

[67] From an article written by Tom Campbell called Primal Male and Female.

My Way Zen

Christmas sermon in York Minster in 2017. Archbishop Sentamu had the whole congregation with their arms out stretched saying God loves me this much. It was a magical moment.

The clearest expression I have found in the Bible of the Father's love for us, is the famous parable of the prodigal son[68].

Parable of the Prodigal Son.

Jesus continued: "There was a man who had two sons. The younger one said to his father, 'Father, give me my share of the estate.' So, he divided his property between them. "Not long after that, the younger son got together all he had, set off for a distant country and there squandered his wealth in wild living. After he had spent everything, there was a severe famine in that whole country, and he began to be in need. He went and hired himself out to feed pigs. He longed to fill his stomach with the pods the pigs were eating, but no one gave him anything. "When he came to his senses, he said, 'How many of my father's hired servants have food to spare, and here I am starving to death! I will set out and go back to my father and say to him: Father, I have sinned against heaven and against you. I am no longer worthy to be called your son; make me like one of your hired servants.' So, he got up and went to his father.

***But while he was still a long way off, his father saw him and was filled with compassion for him**; he ran to his son, threw his arms around him and kissed him. "The son said to him, 'Father, I have sinned against heaven and against you. I am no longer worthy to be called your son.' "But the father said to his servants, 'Quick! Bring the best robe and put it on him. Put a ring on his finger and sandals on his feet. Bring the fattened calf and kill it. Let's have a feast and celebrate. For this son of mine was dead and is alive again; he was lost and is found.[69]*

---

[68] Luke 15:11-32.

[69] The parable continues with the reaction of the elder son. This, I think, is a teaching for the Pharisees as they may think they have never been separated from God.

My Way Zen

The unconditional love of the Father was made real for me when I took the Advanced Christ path with Andrew Harvey[70]. One of the practices Andrew gave us as to visualise yourself as the prodigal son and feel the overwhelming warmth of love of the Father when he rushes out to embrace you. I did this and from that moment, I know we have a loving Father. Try it yourself.

The love of the Creator is so great, there is no need for us to do anything, sacrifices etc., to win the favour of God. This is a KEY understanding. From this you realise Jesus was never a sacrifice. How could a loving father require his son to be tortured and put to death in such a cruel way? No. The crucifixion story requires a different explanation. This is given in the Urantia Book in paper 186 and elsewhere. Please refer to this book for more information.

Part 3 - Purification process

The third part of the covenant in its original formulation was a series of seven vows or commandments - Do not kill, do not steal, do not bear false witness and so on. I noticed most of the commandments apply to one of the seven main chakras. So, in the modern formulation of the covenant, I connected the commandments to these chakras[71] and created a purification process which is set out in appendix 5. I have also extended them to the three main bodies of the VR avatar[72] - mind, body and spirit. In accordance with the philosophy of My Way Zen, you are invited to

---

[70] Andrew Harvey is an amazing man and teacher. I was fortunate to join him on a tour of South India, ending up at the sacred mountain of Arunachala and the ashram of Ramana Maharshi. Andrew is a sacred activist and I thoroughly recommend any and all of his books, programs and courses.

[71] Chakras are energy vortexes or wheels in the subtle energy fields of the body i.e. your VR avatar.

[72] Your "avatar" in the ☐♀VR can be split into Mind, Body and Spirit. The mind can be further broken down into the mental body and emotional body.

generate your own purification process. The one presented here is a summarised version of one that I have developed for myself. It can be modified to suit your own requirements.

The original formulation also included an injunction to spread the word. This was a key consideration at the time of the original covenant. Machiventa Melchizedek obviously wanted the message spread far and wide in what we would nowadays call an evangelical mission. In the modern world, with so many competing religions, my feeling is we don't need a new religion. Consequently, I have excluded from the modern formulation of the covenant anything to do with trying to convert others to your point of view.

The My Way Zen purification process presented in this book is the basic purification process with a brief summary of advanced practices for those of you that would like to take the purification process a step further. If you would like more details of the advanced practices, please email me at **mywayzen@gmail.com**.

Summary of suggested practices

The Purification process is fundamentally about raising your frequency, so that your body can hold more light. Here is a short list of some ideas to raise frequency:

- High vibration diet and alkaline water
- Positive thoughts and affirmations
- Being with positive people
- Reading positive books
- Walks in Nature
- Massage

- Body work such as Yoga, dance and music
- Meditation (and silence)
- Quiet time of contemplation and reflection
- Hypnosis bootcamp program[73]
- Energy work (Prana or Chi) such as Tai Chi and breathing exercises[74].
- Do what brings you joy

Purification

We are living in a virtual reality world with a purpose - to evolve by increasing the quality of our consciousness. This is achieved by raising our frequency and being more loving. This process can be called the Ascension process and involves a series of initiations. At this time, the main one is to purify our body, mind and spirit so we can hold more light and raise our frequency. This is a personal project and my advice is to avoid trying to "convert" anybody else (including your family) to your way of thinking. So, the evangelical message in the original covenant has been revised. The best way of "converting" others is by being a living, loving example.

Revelation

The second part of the process is Revelation or Disclosure. We need disclosure of extra-terrestrials and their involvement in our affairs. This includes disclosure of ET technology. It also includes disclosure of crimes against humanity. We need people in authority to tell us the truth. As Patricia Cori says in her book No More

---

[73] Hypnosis is a powerful way of cutting through obstacles by accessing a deeper part of yourself.

[74] There are many schools for energy work. One that I would like to try is PanEuRhythmy, a system gifted by Beinsa Douno.

My Way Zen

Secrets, No More Lies, we need Disclosure[75].

The Great Mystery

As explained before, the One Creator Being has three personalities:

- God the Father - The Universal Father
- God the Son - The Eternal Son
- God the Holy Spirit - The Infinite Spirit

These are called the Celestials who dwell in Paradise (i.e. the base reality). We are amazing beings. We are worldbridgers[76] and can link from the very centre of creation, the base reality, to this reality here on Earth. This means we are living as a person here on earth, using very similar archetypal programs to the "Son" programs, i.e. we are made in the image of God. This is proved in the incarnation of Christ Michael as a human being that we know as Jesus but was actually called Jeshua. The way this was done is incomprehensible. It is impossible for us to fully understand the nature of the base reality. So fundamentally we are living in a Deep Mystery. The Melchizedek Covenant is fundamentally Mystical[77].

The way back hOMe for me is to follow the path of what I call My Way Zen. We are all unique beings and therefore we each have our own journey. Many pilgrims have been on the journey before. I have borrowed some of their ideas and descriptions to help me (and

---

[75] If you do not know about Disclosure, please checkout Dr Steven Greer, Sirius Disclosure and the film Above Majestic, and many others including Jordan Sather and David Wilcock.

[76] Worldbridger is a word that I first heard from Juliet and Jiva (The Template.org)

[77] Adopting the My Way Zen perspective will make you a Mystic - be careful, as many people can misunderstand this.

with this book, and potentially you as the reader). The path is to follow your heart and do the very best you can. Ultimately you realise there is 'Nothing to do", just move yourself into receive mode in the presence of your Higher Self and receive the ascension codes directly. The Stargate Experience explains it beautifully: "As there is nothing to do, you cannot make a mistake". It is the path of "Faith and Faith alone", the motto of the Melchizedeks. You have a loving Creator. Have faith and you will get through whatever is troubling you.

Black Belt Training

To achieve the very best, advanced students can adopt the black belt level of attainment. I was gifted this explanation of Black Belt attitude when I practiced Kuk Sool Won martial arts training for a brief period.

Black Belt	Warrior of Light
Respect your opponent	Respect others and the environment
Listen to your teachers	Listen to the messages from the Universe - human teachers, animals and synchronicities
Maximum effort	Follow the Joyful Path of Good Fortune and put your heart and soul into your spiritual practice
Confidence, no self	Egoless service to the Will of God

Egoless service to the Will of God is reflected in the PanEuRhythmy prayer "the Ultimate purpose of the Human Soul is to submit to the Will of God".

Melchizedek Priesthood

The Melchizedek priesthood is for those of you who would like to take the next step. You can self-initiate yourself as a Melchizedek, or you could join a school of Melchizedek to train as a Light Priest or Priestess. Please write to me if you are interested.

Melchizedek Teachings

Along with virtually all other spiritual systems here on Earth, the teachings of Melchizedek lineage have been misunderstood and corrupted. So, my advice is always - do you own research and figure out for yourself what is right for you and what is not.

I have often associated the Melchizedek lineage with different symbols and colours: - for example a black and white chequer board pattern or the yin yang tai chi symbol representing the balance of the polarities - Good and Evil, Black and White etc. A key part of seeing the world as a Melchizedek is to understand how the multi-dimensional world appears here on a 3D level as a duality of opposites. All these seeming opposites can be resolved by transcending them and seeing they are just opposite ends of the same thing. For example, at one level we can see this as a fight between Good vs Evil. This fight will continue forever, until we see there is a third force. This third force is Love. This is brilliantly explained by Wesley Tudor Pole[78] in his pamphlet Good vs Evil. Dr David Hawkins also gives a brilliant explanation of transcending the opposites in his master series of talk called The Highest Level of Enlightenment[79].

Another symbol shown in the Urantia book for the Melchizedek

---

[78] Wesley Tudor Pole's books and pamphlets and can be obtained from Chalice Well, Glastonbury, UK.

[79] The Highest Level of Enlightenment are a series of talks given by Dr David Hawkins and produced by Nightingale Conant.

lineage is three concentric rings:

This was the symbol worn by Machiventa Melchizedek. It can be seen as a symbol for the Trinity: Three circles with the same centre. In the centre there is the Void.

Beyond Religion

My Way Zen is beyond religion, politics and war[80]. To go beyond religion, you need to take time to get to know about religion so that you know what you are going beyond. I have noticed that a lot of people are anti-religion but don't know much about it. I feel that there is a danger of throwing the baby out with the bath water. There are a lot of beautiful passages in the Bible revealing profound truths. Unfortunately, there is also the reverse: - mistranslations and misunderstanding, bits removed, and bits added. It has been used by some religionists[81] to make money, gain power or attract celebrity. So, for me, I have studied lots of different religions and found they all contain universal truths. It is time to drop the dogma and for all of us to come together in a universal brotherhood and sisterhood, Beyond Religion.

---

[80] Beyond Poverty, Politics and War is similar to the strap line for Legalise Freedom, an online radio hosted by independent UK writer and journalist Greg Moffitt. It features interviews with some of the World's foremost alternative thinkers and researchers. An archive of 200+ shows is available to stream or download for free.

[81] A religionist or religious zealot, in my view, makes two fundamental mistakes: The first mistake is to believe their beliefs are the right ones and universally true and therefore others are wrong and following on from this, they attempt to convert others to their views.

Freedom and the Luciferian mistake

As explained in the Urantia Book, Lucifer denied the existence of the Universal Father and rebelled against "Paradise" rule. Lucifer thought that he could do a better job than the Divine Plan. He rebelled and instigated the rebellion in 33 systems including Urantia i.e. here on Earth. This is the main reason for the situation we are in. As a rebellion planet we did not receive the benefits that come from following the Divine Plan and have been led astray. In my view, this is not our fault and therefore the idea of Original Sin is incorrect.

Lucifer choose from his own freewill to deny the existence of a Creator. My advice is do not make the same mistake.

Zen Paradox

The path is a bit zen at the end of the day as it is a paradox. The paradox is that by being as humble as you can, you become the Master. By becoming completely free, you become the Servant, a Servant to the Way. The Way leads back to the Universal Father. This is the Divine Plan.

Freedom and surrender

One area that I am working on, is trying to understand the dynamic between the wish to be free, completely liberated and the wish to be of service, to do the Will of God, as an act of surrender. Surrender of your personal will to freedom for the greater good. Initially it seems paradoxical. Contemplating this recently, I realised that I was getting caught up in concepts. After all Freedom is a concept.

My Way Zen

Ultimate Freedom is beyond words and concepts and is the ultimate act of surrender to the Way.

The Way is the way of the Servant Leader. It seems to be a contradiction at first, but in reality, it is the way forward.

CHAPTER 5

Ascension

"And I saw a new heaven and a new earth" Book of Revelation

Ascension is one of the many buzz words that I came across a few years ago. There are many different views about Ascension. My understanding that it is the rapid raising of consciousness from our current level to 5th dimensional consciousness and beyond. This is achieved by raising our vibration or frequency, through letting go of all lower frequency experiences and behaviour. How this manifests in your life is obviously unique to each one of us, from a My Way Zen perspective.

To do this, it helps to have a map of consciousness. The main one I use is the map provided by IODP[82]. Here is a brief summary of the dimensions[83] or layers of density from our 3D layer (the first layer)

---

[82] IODP used to be called the Institute of Divine Potential. After the particle emergence on 21st December 2017 it was renamed Innerversity of Divine Perfection. More details can be found on the IODP website at www.iodp.love. It has many highly recommended programs, such as DNA regenesis and the Ultimate Energy Clearing protocol created by my dear brothers Christof and Sananda.

[83] I use the word dimension and density interchangeably throughout this book. Higher densities can

up to the Avatar layer:

Layer	Density		
First layer (3D)	1st density = Stones, minerals and crystals	2nd density = Plants and animals	3rd density = Self-reflective beings such as Humans
Second layer (Soul)	4th density = Dream like consciousness	5th density = Unconditional love	6th density = I Am That I Am
Third layer (Monad)	7th density - the Self merges with the Infinite	8th density - There is no self	9th density = Causeless Being of Love
Fourth layer (Avatar)	10th =?	11th =?	12th =?

There are even higher states of consciousness eg the Rishi levels 13th to 15th, but these are so far above where we are now, they are impossible to explain at our current level of consciousness. So, I have left them out of the above table. Even the Avataric level of being is beyond most of our understanding, so I have just put a ? for the different densities within the Fourth layer[84].

We are currently at 3rd density in our waking state and experience part of the 4th density during our dream state. We are collectively on the verge of a major shift to the 5th density consciousness. This

---

manifest in this VR as "physical" or as non-physical phenomena.

[84] The Stargate Experience offers many programs, such as their youthing program (telomeres lengthened, mitochondria increased and so on). It uses 12th dimensional energy based on actual or etheric stargates. If you want to experience 12th dimensional energy, please sign up for one of their courses.

is where we become unconditionally loving beings in a Golden Age. New chakras in our body become activated[85] and we manifest our new race genetic in bodily form.

Law of attraction

The idea of raising your frequency fits in with another New Age buzz word - the law of attraction. The basis of the law of attraction is like attracts like. So, if you wish to attract into your life a partner, or money or something else, you need to vibrate at the frequency of what you wish to attract. The higher, the better.

There are numerous books and views on the law of attraction such as The Secret. Most of them appear to be based on "getting more stuff", so I tend to avoid them. However, Joe Dispenza's has a series of books and courses which appear to avoid the pitfalls of using the law of attraction for personal gain.

Evolution

Another way of understanding Ascension is a rapid evolution in consciousness rather like a state transition in physics. An analogy could be water being heated up. It takes time for the water temperature to rise (evolution). When it hits boiling point, it suddenly changes its form or state from liquid to gas or steam (ascension).

Being and Becoming

Many years ago, I was a student of Evolutionary Spirituality, an

---

[85] The new chakras are the 8th Chakra called the Krystos or Higher heart. It is the source of unconditional love. We will still have our lower heart, the 4th chakra which is about personal love.

online course with Craig Hamilton, a student of Andrew Cohen. One of the many great insights that Andrew Cohen and later Craig offered me, is that there are two principles underlying your life: Being and Becoming:

- Being as the fundamental nature of everything, the Ground of Being
- Becoming as the fundamental drive in all life to grow - to grow in complexity and become what is intended, the Greeks called this the Telos[86].

I believe the Telos for a human being is the Ascension path to Perfection. As Jesus said to "Be ye perfect as my father in Heaven is perfect"[87]. This drive can be called the evolutionary impulse. The key message of Evolutionary Spirituality is that we need both Being and Becoming to awaken to the Authentic Self. Andrew Cohen points out that one of the many "misunderstandings" of the ancient Indian systems is the concept of Enlightenment, which is taken to be reaching the place of pure Being. This is a place of perfection where you do not need to do anything as everything is seen as perfect just as it is. Reaching this place, is a huge spiritual achievement, but is not the end of the journey. The remainder of journey is to bring the realisations and higher states of consciousness into the "market place"[88]. To live the truth of who

---

[86] Telos is a Greek word for the purpose or reason for something. For example, the Telos for an acorn is to become an oak tree. I love trees and it is a constant amazement how a small acorn has within it all the information needed to create such a magnificent tree as an oak tree. The timescales differ for different trees. For example, an oak tree can grow to full size within a few hundred years. We humans also have a telos - to compete the journey hOMe and become one with the celestial beings at the centre. An acorn may accomplish its telos within a few hundred years. We may take many many lifetimes to accomplish ours.

[87] Matthew 5:48.

My Way Zen

you are, in every moment wherever you are. If we stopped at the stage of bliss, and did not get off our meditation cushion, then we have missed the point.

After experiencing the Great Perfection[89], when you come back into the world, you find that it is riddled with issues - just about everything needs a major reset: Financial systems, where there are a few hugely wealthy people and the rest of us living in relative poverty - this is not how it was meant to work; Environmental destruction on a vast scale; Loss of bio-diversity leading to possibly the 6th mass extinction event; Health systems with obesity and other modern diseases like diabetes on the increase; Education systems that are not serving the needs of the Indigo and other children; undemocratic political systems like the European commission; energy systems that are polluting the planet (fossil fuels, nuclear and other systems). The list goes on and on and as I mentioned in the forward, I plan to write a book on the Global Reset, which will cover all these issues and more, along with possible solutions. Just know that virtually all our current issues can be solved, when we get access to the ET technology that is being kept secret from us by the Deep State.

So, getting off the meditation cushion and entering the world is quite an experience. It is helped by having access to both the Being and Becoming aspects. Maharishi[90] called it living at 200%

---

[88] Like the final picture in the ox herding series of teachings.

[89] The Buddhist system that concentrates on the Great Perfection is called Dzogchen.

[90] The great Mahesh Maharishi yogi provided us with so many gifts including Transcendental meditation. I remember one of his teaching very clearly when he explained that awakened consciousness was like having 200% consciousness. Aware and living 100% of the small self (the becoming aspect) and the 100% of the Big Picture consciousness - Big Mind (Genpo Roshi) or Cosmic awareness - both at the same time i.e. 200%.

consciousness.

Diamond Light

It is truly a gift to be able to be in service to the great unfolding, the Ascension. To be here at this time and experiencing the waves of high frequency light currently bathing the Earth. One of the latest waves is called the Diamond Light wave and was introduced to the planet on solstice June 21st, 2018. More details of this can be found at Era of Peace[91].

Evolutionary Impulse and Desire

The Evolutionary Impulse, when fully experienced, feels like rocket fuelled desire or ambition to evolve. In the Buddhist teachings desire gets a bad rap. For example, the four noble truths taught by Buddha are sometimes presented as:

- Life is suffering (Dukha)
- Suffering is caused by desire
- There is an end to suffering
- The path that leads to the end of suffering

This version of Buddha's teachings often puts the "blame" of suffering on desire[92]. The idea is to somehow remove all desires and

---

[91] Era of Peace is the website of Patricia Cota Robles who provides really beautifully weekly vlogs. For me, these have been extremely powerful ways of connecting to the I Am presence within me and within all of Humanity. The vlogs that stand out for me are vlog37 and vlog68 on the Diamond light. The Diamond light is summarised at appendix 12.

[92] Other translations have ignorance or attachment instead of desire. Ignorance is the better

My Way Zen

then you will be happy and free from suffering. When I tried to put this into practice, I realised that you get caught in a trap: the desire for enlightenment, for ascension, for liberation, to be free from suffering, is itself a desire. I was caught in the paradox: The desire to remove all desires. However, there is a solution which I have presented in the Four Bodhisattva vows - see Appendix 8 for details.

Initiations on the Christ Path

Another way of understanding Ascension is that it is the process of taking initiations. The path through the initiations will be unique to you (your My Way Zen path).

The initiations can come in the form of realisations (Satori) or physical events. The realisations are usually followed by the hard work of integrating them into your system, your bit of Q♀VR.

The sequence of initiations presented here is based on the life story of Jesus, the great master.

Initiation 1 - Birth as Christ
Initiation 2 - Baptism
Initiation 3 - Transfiguration[93]
Initiation 4 - Crucifixion
Initiation 5 - Resurrection
Initiation 6 - Ascension

---

translation, in my view. When ignorance is dispelled, we will see things are they really are. We will see how our actions create karma. Our ignorance of karma and how Q♀VR works is, I believe, the main cause of our suffering.

[93] Some people present the Transfiguration as the first initiation because the first two in the list above are viewed as preliminaries.

My Way Zen

The first initiation "the Birth as Christ" is when you realise that you (and everyone else) is part of Christ. You are a Christ being and you are "born again". This is often followed by a lengthy purification process leading up to the second initiation, the baptism by the Holy Spirit. This was a big moment in the life of Jesus. In the Urantia book, the order of events is slightly different to that presented in the Bible. The 40 days in the wilderness occurred before the Baptism[94] and not after it.

The Baptism of Christ by Piero della Francesca

The beautiful and powerful painting reveals Jesus as the master of the wisdom of the Dove[95]. The next initiation after the Baptism is

the Transfiguration (or Metamorphosis). This is when Jesus appeared in a radiant form to a select group of disciples on Mount

---

[94] The Baptism is explained in the Urantia Book as the moment when Jesus's mortal mind merged with his Higher Self (or thought adjuster using UB's terminology).

[95] Matthew 10:16 "Behold, I am sending you out as sheep in the midst of wolves, so be wise as serpents and innocent as doves".

Hermon[96]. This will be a huge initiation for us, when we accomplish this, acquire a new bodily form and we become the Radiant ones.

The New Race Genetic

As part of the ascension process, we may be gifted an upgrade to our physical body (i.e. our avatar in the $\male\female$VR). There are lots of different words for this upgraded body, but I believe they are all referring to the same thing. Nobody really knows what this upgrade will be as it will be the first time on Earth that it has manifested, apart from in the case of Jesus. However, the coding is hidden within our DNA, so we will just be remembering how we used to be. Names for the new race genetic for our body (avatar) are:

- 5th dimensional Crystalline[97] solar light body
- Morontia body (Urantia Book's word for the ascended body)
- Adam Kadmon light body
- Homo Divinicus (Openhand)
- Homo Universalis (Barbara Marx Hubbard)
- Homo Spiritualis
- I Am Avatar[98]
- Homo Luminous
- Superhuman OS 2.0
- MerKaBa (Chariot of fire)
- Golden Race[99]

---

[96] See Urantia Book paper 158 The Mount of Transfiguration.

[97] Crystalline in the sense that it will be a mixture of carbon and silicon. Silicon is the main component of glass - and computer chips. Silicon is the next level up from carbon on the periodic table - from an atomic weight of 6 to 14.

[98] I Am Avatar ie part of the I Am Race - an anagram of America

[99] The Golden Age could have been mis translated and actually mean the arrival of a Golden Race.

My Way Zen

- Human angelic diamond sun DNA template
- Homo Deus (Yuval Noah Harini)
- Omega Man/Woman (Group of Forty)
- Most sacred body or supercelestial body (Sufism)
- Rainbow body (Tibetan Buddhism)
- Diamond body (Taoist)
- Body of bliss (Kriya yoga)
- The Divine body (Yogic/Tantra)
- Super conductive body (Vedanta)
- Luminous body (Egyptian)
- Radiant body (Gnostics)
- Perfect body (Mithraism)
- Immortal body (Hermetic teachings)
- Golden body (Alchemical and emerald tablets)

This body will have enhanced psychic powers, including telepathy; the ability to see the Quantum; and many more amazing abilities including perhaps the ability to rejuvenate[100]. So, we are on the cusp of a major uplift in not only our consciousness but also our consciousness as it is expressed in the world.

Ascension groups and the Harvest

There are different views on who will ascend. My view is based on the Law of One books. These envisage the Harvest as three groups[101]:

---

[100] The rejuvenation technology will give us quasi immortality or become a-mortal as envisaged by Yuval Noah Hariri in his book Homo Deus i.e. we can still die through war or an accident. This is a controversial subject as we need to a major change in our behaviour, including birth control where only elected couples would be allowed to have given birth to new humans.

[101] Law of One: Session 65 (page 109 of book 3): RA: "I am Ra. Among planetary harvest which yield a

My Way Zen

ASCENSION GROUPS

Choices	Comments
Ascension group	The Ascension group are those of us who want to raise our frequency and therefore the amount of light we can hold, by following a spiritual practice. For me this is the My Way Zen path. We are each unique, therefore our paths will be different. If you are reading this book, my guess is you are in the Ascension group, particularly if you took the "red pill".
Middle group	I call this group the sleepwalkers. This group does not appear to like change and seems to be happy with a level of complacency in the face of so many issues. I am not sure whether sleepwalkers see what is happening all around them, or feel powerless and choose to ignore it: the environmental damage, the corporate greed agenda, the military-corporate-industrial complex, the corruption in politics, in the corporate world like the pharmaceutical companies, the pollution from the oil and gas industry, corruption in the financial system, in our law courts, in the police and so on.

harvest of mind/body/spirit complexes approximately 10% are negative; approximately 60% are positive; and approximately 30% are mixed with nearly all harvest being positive.

My Way Zen

	This group may also include those who are waking up but have not made a decision on which way to go. Perhaps they do not even realise that there is a decision to be made? I guess it includes those that decide to take the blue pill and not the red pill.
Negative Agenda Beings	This group follows the Luciferian agenda or some other negative agenda. I know this may sound weird, but Lucifer is a key player in all this. There was a rebellion about 200,000 years ago and we "fell" and are now in a forced evolution system of domination and control. More details of this are in the Urantia Book and at appendix 7. For whatever reason, those beings who have chosen this group want to live in their own hell of a "mad max" world as survivors in some post-apocalyptic world, perhaps to balance their karma.

One test as to whether you are in the Ascension group in the Law of One material is whether you are living with at least 50% of your time in service to others. It is not saying you have to be like Jesus and spend every single moment in service to others. You can spend a portion of your time about your own affairs, but at least 50% of your waking life is about looking after others. A lot of so called "work" can fall into this category. However, if you are only working for the money, then probably you are not using your job as an opportunity to serve others. You can make your own judgement here.

An alternative way of understanding whether you are in the Ascension group is to follow the test in the Melchizedek Covenant of "Faith and Faith alone". Accordingly, just by having faith in your

My Way Zen

Creator and being harmless[102] will be sufficient for you to be redeemed and brought into the Ascension.

Negative Agenda Beings

Other names for the Negative Agenda Beings are: Left spin, dark lodge, lunar lords, black hats, bad actors, the Cabal, the dark ones, the Deep State, the Illuminati and so on. They are like a parasite or virus that has entered our Virtual Reality. Part of the Ascension process is raising the frequency which will act like an "anti-virus" software. These beings will no longer be able to operate here and will leave when the separation of densities takes place and will leave.

Unconditional Love

The Ascension can also be thought of as a higher level of consciousness, a more loving and compassionate way of being in the world. I have been a follower of Matt Kahn for some time and love watching his talks on YouTube. He explains 5th dimensional consciousness as being unconditionally loving. All experiences, including the so-called negative ones, are seen with loving eyes as yet another opportunity to learn to love, to surrender[103] to the "what is".

---

[102] Be Harmless is the main injunction in my modern version of the Melchizedek Covenant. This means causing as little harm as possible to yourself, other human beings, animals and the environment. It is also the main requirement of One Earth Nation and a key teaching of Buddha Maitreya the Christ.

[103] I love the way lots of great spiritual ideas are portrayed so well in films. One such case is in the 8th, the latest film in the Star Wars saga. Luke Skywalker, the Last Jedi, in the end disappears. My guess is that this is the ultimate surrender and from this place, the next film will show how he overcomes the "Dark Side" by transcendence.

To get to this place, the starting point is always yourself - loving yourself. If you cannot love yourself, then it is unlikely that you can fully love the world and enter 5th dimensional loving consciousness. When you experience unity, you realise you and the world are one - You are IT.

The Joyful Path of Good Fortune

The Joyful Path of Good Fortune is the name of a book by Geshe Kelsang Gyatso[104] and contains the Kadampa path in three books. It is also the name I like to give the path or journey hOMe.

Follow the My Way Zen path and you will be following the path of joy, peace and harmony, the joyful path of Good Fortune.

Synchronicities, and messages from the Universe provide all the support you need on the journey. This is abundance. Abundance is not lots of money. It is having what you need to do the things you need to do[105].

When you follow the path, you will find it full of synchronicities and all the support you need. I sometimes call the path "the Next Step practice". You will not be given all the steps to take as it would be too much. Instead you are given the next step. You will only find out what the next step after that is, when you have taken the next step. If you do not take this step, you will never find out what the path was. You will miss the opportunity, the Kairos moment. The

---

[104] Geshe Kelsang Gyatso (Geshe la) was the spiritual director of the New Kadampa Tradition (NKT).

[105] Thank you Darryl Anka (Bashar) for this gem.

82

My Way Zen

process is to surrender the ego mind, the controlling small mindset and trust that you will be led to where you need to go. If you follow this practice, you will be guided by your Higher Self. Your Higher Self can see the big picture and will create a beautiful life for you, often way more amazing than anything your small-minded ego could think up.

Of course, sometimes you can misread the signs and take the wrong turn. When this happens, it is still a learning experience. With practice and with purification of your sensory system, it becomes easier and easier to listen to higher guidance. The next step becomes obvious. Take it. You will not regret it.

CHAPTER **6**

The Journey hOMe

"I am the Way and the Truth and the Life" John 14:6

So, we have got to the last chapter in this book. You hopefully are now on the spiritual path and making the journey back hOMe. Where is hOMe you might ask? Well the Zen answer is right **here and now**.

The Zen Way home

The Zen way of understanding the way hOMe is in many of the koans and teachings. The one that I have chosen as an example is a simple but profound discussion between Zhaozhou (Joshu) and one of his early teachers Nanquan (Nansen). This is reported in the book Making Zen Your Own as follows:

It is a famous exchange, the first one in The Recorded Sayings of Zen Master Joshu as well as koan 19 in The Gateless Gate, translated by the late Koun Yamada Rishi:

"What is the Way?" Joshu earnestly asked Nansen.

My Way Zen

Nansen answered, "The ordinary mind is the Way."
Joshu asked, "Should I direct myself toward it or not?"
Nansen said, "If you try to turn towards it, you go against it."
Joshu asked "If I do not try to turn toward it, how can I know that it is the
Way?"
Nansen answered, "The Way does not belong to knowing or not knowing.
Knowing is delusion; not-knowing is a blank consciousness. When you have
reached the true Way beyond all doubt, you will find it as vast and boundless as
the great empty firmament. How can it be talked about on the level of being the
right or wrong Way?"[106]

So, the Way - the Tao - the journey hOMe - is Ordinary Mind! and you cannot direct or control it, rather the way is to surrender to the Infinite and enter the zero point.[107]

Urantia Book

If you would like a more complicated way of understanding the journey hOMe, you can find it in the Urantia Book. We are on our journey back to our Creator - the Trinity being(s) in Paradise. The journey goes something like this: You first need to graduate from Urantia and become a galactic citizen. When you have evolved sufficiently through many lives in the capital of the local system (Satania), you can progress to the capital of the galaxy and finally to Salvington, the capital of the local universe. After completing our training there, you can be elected to make the journey to the Super Universe, the universe of universes, the original universe for all the VR universes in our type of universe (one with the full Trinity:

---

[106] From page 91 and 92 in Making Zen Your Own, by Janet Abels (see Bibliography)

[107] The zero-point field is outside time and space as pure consciousness - not identified with anything. It is also called the Sacred Neutral or the Void. The zero-point field holds pure potential and the bliss codes for the full enjoyment of this embodiment.

My Way Zen

Father, Son and Spirit). You will be a very high dimensional being at this stage and ready to make the final journey to the very centre Havona. At the very centre of Havona is Paradise. I am not sure what happens there, but it will be amazing.

On our journey to the Centre, the next step is graduation from Urantia. This will be accomplished by Ascension. The method was demonstrated by Jesus when he appeared in his ascended body after the resurrection. In the Urantia Book this body is called the Morontia[108] body. We know that we can go this far, right to the very centre, because of the incarnation of Christ Michael in human form (Jesus), here on Urantia. We have the same apparatus (the human DNA body suit) that Jesus had, albeit he was able to switch on the full DNA sequence of codes in his body. We currently have a "dumbed down" version.

We each have what the Urantia Book calls as a thought adjuster. This is your unique Divine spark or God fragment. It is basically a connection to the Base reality (Paradise). Do not ask me how this works as I don't know, all you need to know is that you can communicate directly with the central Paradise being (the Universal Father). This communication channel becomes fully operational when you complete the initiation and purification process, as it did for Jesus when he declared "I and my Father are One"[109].

---

[108] Morontia is the name of another type of virtual reality which has 200 elements, compared with the 100 elements here, ignoring unstable radioactive ones. Apparently, some of the Morontia elements are available here. I believe that one of them is monoatomic gold. This is white gold that has gone through a process to become partly multi-dimensional. There are apparently 570 levels of the Morontia body. The first 8 levels can manifest in this virtual reality. Jesus appeared in his ascended form 19 times, during which time he revealed all 8 types.

[109] John 10:30

As Jesus explained, but was so often misunderstood, the Kingdom lies within each of us. The journey is an inward journey, to higher and higher levels of consciousness. It not an external kingdom. We are connected, like he was, directly to God (via the thought adjuster). Each one of us is infinitely precious and this planet is sacred beyond measure.

Unity and the Void

Oneness and its relationship to the Void could do with a chapter all on its own. I will try to explain it, knowing it is beyond words, beyond the mind and yet all around you as Ordinary Mind.

You are All that you see[110], you are living in your bubble of reality, dreaming it all into existence from the collective information source field. Unity consciousness is seeing it is all one system - one holographic virtual reality: Q♀VR. It has a unique quality, we are all loved by our Creator, the system runs on Love. I know we have a loving Mother/Father Creator. The source of the creative energy lies within you, in your hara or womb[111]. The womb is dark and it's the source of everything. Pure potential. The Void. Nothing. The Zen place of not knowing, the realisation of "Not this", Advaita or Non-dual Consciousness.

---

[110] Tim Freke gives a lot of good advice on how to do this by "stepping back" and experiencing the Oneness. Douglas Harding also provides another quick method to experience this in his book "On Having No Head".

[111] The womb exists in both male and female bodies. There is one basic DNA human body suit which is used to create both male and female forms. The X/Y chromosomes allow the sexual organs to manifest differently. So, men have nipples, but the breast flesh is not made as big as those in a female (but there are men boobs). Women can sometimes have facial hair. Then the two testicles become the two ovaries, the penis is inside a woman and its tip (the most sensitive bit) is the clitoris and finally the womb in a man is very small but is energetically there as the Hara.

Lots of words - pointing to the place that is not a place. Sorry, I cannot give you any better directions. Just sit in silence for however long it takes. One day you will experience it. It is the end of suffering, the end of doubt. It is the Perfection; The Ground of Being; Source consciousness; directly connected to the highest levels within the matrix and beyond.

Kingdom within

The kingdom within has many names. The ones I like are the Holy of Holies, the Cup, the Holy Grail[112], the crystalline chamber of the Heart, or simply Xanadu, my name for this place. To get there you need to enter the Void. The place of nothing -no thing with infinite potential. It is infinitely dark, but at the same time filled with light. It is initially reached through meditation. With practice it can become an everyday experience.

A great description of light within the darkness is in a poem by Elizabeth Jennings which I have reproduced in appendix 11 - A World of Light.

The place can also be called the Sacred Neutral. Here all opposites are transcended, and you rest in the Sacred Neutral as the observer, witnessing the 'What is", the Q♀VR with no desires, in non-judgement, in sacred union and communion with Infinite Intelligence. This is like "standing on the shoreline of Infinity".[113]

---

[112] Please see appendix 13 - The Quest for the Holy Grail.

[113] Robert Moss, I believe, is the source of this great description of the state of consciousness described in this chapter. The other one I like is the Active side of Infinity. The source for this one is Carlos Casteneda.

My Way Zen

For those of you who like to know about metaphysics, the Void is a black hole that connects to the Sun and the Sun behind the Sun, the Galactic central sun, and so on until you reach Base Reality. There are two main toroidal magnetic fields[114] that are generated in the Heart chakra. When the centres of the two fields come into alignment, you get to experience the Union of Opposites, the Christ Majesty, and the unconditional LOVE of the God Source, the Omega light, the Ain Soph.

It is now up to you, what do you choose to do?

The journey can be as long or as short as determined by your Unique Self. My advice is to start the journey now. As the old Chinese saying goes: "A journey of a thousand miles begins with a single step".

May you be blessed on your joyful path of Good Fortune.

---

[114] According to Heartmath, the heart generates magnetic fields which are much more powerful than those generated by the brain. The centre of the toroidal field, the black hole, could be thought of as a stargate or access point to the rest of the universe.

Epilogue

It was the fashion to have an epilogue, for those who want a little bit more. The epilogue that I like best is the one in my favourite play - the Midsummers Night's Dream by The Bard[115]:

> *"If we shadows have offended,*
> *Think but this, and all is mended,*
> *That you have but slumber'd here*
> *While these visions did appear.*
> *And this weak and idle theme,*
> *No more yielding but a dream,*
> *Gentles, do not reprehend:*
> *if you pardon, we will mend"*

For the epilogue to this book, I thought I would mention a personal aspect of my path. Anybody who knows anything about Zen, knows that knowledge is delusion. With that said, for me personally, my journey hOMe has included a process of accumulating lots of knowledge. Perhaps, this is because I will need to take an examination when I graduate from Urantia. My idea for the exam is that it is called Conspiracy Theory (Expert). It can cover almost any (esoteric) topic: from ascension to sacred geometry, from the architecture of this reality to Xanadu, from the Adam Kadmon body, to world history and timelines, Pyramid technology, DNA and merkaba mechanics, Knights Templars and the Mystery schools, modern science and superintelligence, new financial systems such as cryptocurrency or moneyless systems such as Ubuntu[116]. You name it, the exam could be on anything to do with

---

[115] The Bard is of course William Shakespeare. This name could have been an alias for Francis Bacon, the son of Queen Elizabeth (and the Earl of Leicester) according to Raymond W Bernard in his book The Great Secret Count of St. Germain (1966) which is a fascinating read.

My Way Zen

the Ascension process and the journey hOMe. Consequently, I seem to have become addicted to acquiring more and more knowledge contained in the great teachings and scriptures as well as knowledge about modern physics; artificial intelligence and time travel; pyramid technology; sacred geometry; extra-terrestrials[117]; world history and the new archaeological discoveries in Antarctica and so on.

But I know deep down that all that matters is LOVE. Love yourself and love others, forgive and do not judge, be pro-life, live in gratitude, be in service to others and not service to self, prefer the truth to lies and deception, love not fear, freedom not slavery and above all surrender to the Will of the Father. As my dear brother Sananda says, the path is simple but that does not mean that it is always easy. This is beautifully encapsulated in the Source Declaration:

"I intend to serve my God-Source with my full divine power, absolutely, unconditionally, completely. I am whole. I am sovereign. I am free"[118].

Thank you, Thank you, Thank you.

---

[116] In my view there will be global financial reset at some point. Fiat currency systems have a 100% failure rate. There are a few candidates to replace the existing system such as 1. a gold backed currency issued by the Nation and not a banker's cartel (i.e. a central bank); 2. cryptocurrency (ie a currency "policed" by artificial intelligence); 3. a Quantum Financial System or even; 4. a moneyless society envisioned by Michael Tellinger, called Ubuntu or Contributionism.

[117] More correctly our brothers and sisters from the stars.

[118] Please see Appendix 14 for an explanation of the Source Declaration.

Bibliography

The Big TOE

The Big Theory of Everything (Big TOE) is the main opus of Tom Campbell. It is actually three books in one: Awakening; Discovery; and Inner Workings. The book is a sizeable tome but is mostly an easy read with many amusing asides. However, for most people a more accessible way of getting to grips with the Theory is to watch the many videos on youtube[119] where Tom Campbell explains the Theory and its many applications to life issues.

ISBN 978-09725094-6-6

Urantia Book

The Urantia Book is a compilation of papers given to Humanity by various beings from the Galaxy and Universe. Each paper contains a huge body of information and it will take many years to fully grasp it (if this is possible at all). It was transmitted in the 1920s and 1930s in English but not published until 1955. It uses concepts and ideas that prevailed at the time. Appendix 7 contains more details about this amazing book.

ISBN 978-0911560-51-0

---

[119] The channel name on YouTube for the Big TOE is simply called Tom Campbell.

9 Keys

9 Keys is a powerful program offered by IODP.[120] It covers each chakra in depth (section 3 to 9) with the first two sections being the preliminary practices of purity and centredness.

I am not aware that this has been published. I attended the 9 Keys course and was given my copy of this amazing book at the course. My good friend Athena Melchizedek has summarised the information in her powerful book The Quantum Keys

ISBN 9 781504 377218

Law of One

A lot of the material for DW's talks comes from the Law of One. This is an amazing series of books based on information provided via a method that I first came across with Edgar Cayce[121] and Dolores Cannon. It is called deep regression which is similar to sleep. The process is to put a human being into a deeply regressed state and for that person (the "vessel") to be contacted by beings that are not in physical form. This is not the same as channelling[122]

---

[120] IODP used to be called the Institute of Divine potential and that is the name organisation that produced the 9key program. After particle emergence IODP was renamed the Innerversity of Divine Perfection.

[121] Edgar Cayce was called the sleeping prophet as he made his readings while sleeping. By a remarkable "coincidence" David Wilcock looks like Edgar Cayce.

[122] Channelling happens when someone is awake and taken over by another being. The problem with channelling is that the identity of the being can be anybody.

as the vessel is unconscious or asleep. The Being that provided the Law of One material calls itself Ra and could be a member of the Guardian Alliance that recently helped us through the latest series of upgrades.

ISBN 978-089865-260-4 (This is the ISBN for book I. There are 5 books altogether in the series)

Making Zen Your Own

The name My Way Zen was inspired by a brilliant book by Janet Abels called Making Zen Your Own[123]. The book has a chapter on twelve of the key Chinese Zen masters during the time of the Golden Age of Zen in China (500-900s AD). I thoroughly recommend reading this book. There are numerous stories of the great masters in the book, some of which turn in koans. This book inspired me to make my own form of Zen.

ISBN 978-086171-702-6

Source Field Investigations and Ascension Mysteries

David Wilcock has written a number of books and there is a new one expected to be published soon. The two main books are Source Field Investigations and Ascension Mysteries. They cover a lot of DW's investigation work into the mysteries of the source field. Both books are recommended reading.

Source Field Investigations ISBN 978-0-525-95204-6

---

[123] Making Zen your Own, Giving Life to the Twelve Key Golden Ancestors by Janet Jiryu Abels

My Way Zen

Ascension mysteries ISBN 978-028564-362-8

Alien Interview

The Alien Interview is a very interesting document prepared by a nurse at the Roswell Incident. The nurse (Matilda O'Donnell MacElroy) was able to communicate with the alien telepathically. Matilda managed to retain the transcripts of her "conversations" with the alien. She had been sworn to secrecy, so she did not release the information until the end of her life. She sent them to Lawrence R Spencer, who published them. They make very interesting reading. You can find a copy of the book on Amazon.

Deluxe study edition ISBN 0557130743

The Holographic Universe

The Holographic Universe is a must-read book by Michael Talbot. It is based on the work of Karl Pribham (the brain as a hologram) and David Bohm (the cosmos as a hologram – implicate order). It also contains numerous examples of holograms at work. The ones that intrigued me were the examples of people who can see holographically. Some of the examples that you can check out are: Barbara Brennan; Carol Dryer; Dolores Krieger; Beatrice Rich; Emmanuel Swedenborg and many more.

ISBN 978-0-586-09171-5

Biocentrism

Biocentrism by Robert Lanza with Bob Berman, has a lot of great information about consciousness, quantum physics and the shift in worldview. From the book: "It takes one of the key tenets of

My Way Zen

Western thinking: that all life ultimately reduces to physics. In its place it offers the revolutionary view that biology is primary – that life creates the universe, not the other way around."

While the book has much to recommend it, in my view, it does not go far enough. For example, in the fourth principle of Biocentrism: "Without consciousness, "matter" dwells in an undetermined state of probability. Any universe that could have preceded consciousness only existed in a probability state". This may give the reader the impression that "matter" exists somewhere. Under the virtual reality interpretation, "matter" does not exist and never existed. If you wanted to ascribe some level of existence to it, you could say it exists as information.

ISBN 978-1-935-25174-3

Appendix 1 – My Way Zen sangha and resources

A sangha for My Way Zen has been created. Sangha is one of the three precious jewels in Buddhism: - Buddha, Dharma and Sangha. The sangha is a community of fellow practitioners. The My Way Zen sangha has a website at **www.mywayzen.wildapricot.org**. If you would like to join the sangha and receive regular newsletters and other information, including the resources mentioned in this book, please become a member of the website. The instructions to become a member can be found on the website.

The sangha has a My Way Zen service booklet which contains the ceremonies and prayers to use as a member of the sangha. If you would like a copy, please become a member of the site and then you can access the private pages. The service booklet contains various ceremonies that were "downloaded" by me, including the sacred anointment, sacred baptism and a Zen Eucharist. Some of these have been copied (with permission) from the Wild Goose Sangha including the four Bodhisattva vows which are discussed in Appendix 8.

The resources on the website will also include:

1. Free downloadable meditations and transmissions
2. Free artwork - the blue avian phoenix
3. [Free recipes and suggestions for a high vibration diet]
4. Links to the online courses mentioned in this book.

My Way Zen

Appendix 2 – Original Melchizedek Covenant

The original form of the covenant is set out in the Urantia Book in paper 93 section 4.

1. I believe in El Elyon, the Most High God, the only Universal Father and Creator of all things.
2. I accept the Melchizedek covenant with the Most High, which bestows the favour of God on my faith, not on sacrifices and burnt offerings.
3. I promise to obey the seven commandments of Melchizedek and to tell the good news of this covenant with the Most High to all men.

The seven commandments of the Salem religion[124] were:
1. You shall not serve any God but the Most High Creator of heaven and earth
2. You shall not doubt that faith is the only requirement for eternal salvation
3. You shall not bear false witness
4. You shall not kill
5. You shall not steal
6. You shall not commit adultery
7. You shall not show disrespect for your parents and elders

This Covenant was formulated by Machiventa Melchizedek for the Salem school. As explained in the Urantia Book, Machiventa

---

[124] The Salem religion refers to the teachings of Machiventa Melchizedek when he taught Abram and others from a place called Salem (now Jerusalem). The idea was to prepare the world for the bestowal of Christ Michael (Jesus). Unfortunately, the teachings quickly became corrupted and Machiventa was worshipped almost as a God even though he specifically said there was only One God and that is El Elyon, the Most High.

98

My Way Zen

materialised a body, his avatar in this Q♀VR. This is why the Bible comments that he had no parents[125]. His status was of course misunderstood by the primitive people at that time. He is sometimes portrayed as the "Lord" or a "god". But Machiventa is just a Melchizedek, a very powerful being, but not God.

---

[125] Hebrews 7:3 "Without father, without mother, without descent, having neither beginning of days, nor end of life."

My Way Zen

Appendix 3 – Koan practice

Contemplating koans is one of the fun Zen practices. The idea is to experience the similar realisation that the Zen master had when the koan was created. My source for koans is Dogen's 300 which is compilation of koans from the Gateless gate and Blue Cliff record. You can download the book for free as a pdf. Here is an example:

Number 122 - Fayan's Fire God

Baoen was once studying in the community of Fayan. One day Fayan said, "How long have you been with us?"

Baoen said, "I've been in your community for three years."

Fayan said, "You are a junior person in the monastery. How come you never ask questions?"

Baoen said, "I don't want to mislead you. I must confess. When I was with Master Yuezhou, I attained the peaceful bliss."

Fayan said, "By what words did you enter that place?"

Baoen replied, "When I asked Master Yuezhou, 'What is the self of the practitioner?' he said, 'The fire god seeks fire.'"

Fayan said, "Good words, but I'm afraid you didn't understand them."

Baoen said, "The fire god belongs to fire, fire seeking fire is just like the self seeking self."

Fayan said, "Indeed, you didn't understand. If the Buddhadharma were like that, it wouldn't have come down to this day."

Fayan said, "Why don't you ask me?"

Baoen then said, "What is the self of the practitioner?"

Fayan said, "The fire god seeks fire."

At that, Baoen experienced a great awakening.

So, what is going on here. Fayan as the Zen master was challenging the student Baoen: Does he have the Zen perspective? My comment would be, first of all, the statement "the Fire god seeks

My Way Zen

fire" has within it a contradiction as the Fire god is Fire, so does not seek. Just like the self is Self, so cannot seek it. Secondly as a virtual reality, there is no Fire God, similarly there is no Self. That is the great awakening.

Appendix 4 – List of names for the "End Times"

- Golden Age time lines
- The Great Awakening
- Shift of the Ages
- The Shift
- Times of Prophecy
- The Apocalypse
- Time of Tribulations
- The End Times
- New Age
- New Earth (or Terranova)
- Time of Revelations
- Ascension time
- Tipping point
- Samvartika Fire
- The Times of Noah
- Singularity
- New Jerusalem

- Age of Authenticity
- The Great Unravelling
- The Day of Wrath
- Dies Irae
- Day of Reckoning
- Judgment Day
- Age of Aquarius
- Omega Point
- The Time of the Golden Race
- The Great Revealing
- Ragnarok
- Eschaton
- Fraso Kreti
- The Last Judgment
- The Great Remembering
- Heaven on Earth
- Day of Atonement

Please note, by "The End Times', it is meant the end of one Age and the start of another.

My Way Zen

Appendix 5 – My Way Zen Purification

The My Way Zen purification process is based on the 7 chakras[126] and the 3 bodies - Mind, Body, Spirit.

My advice is to start with the first three chakras: The root chakra (survival); the sacral chakra (sex and passion); and solar plexus (power). These are the ones that need the most clean-up work. When you have made significant progress with these, then move onto the higher chakras.

I have summarised each chakra in a table box. Each box has a description in bold. These are:

Original form of injunction - this links back to the original form of the Melchizedek covenant - see appendix 2 for details.
Location: The location within the body.
Indian name: For those of you that like to refer back to the ancient knowledge, I have included the name from the Indian system.
Colour: Associated colour of the chakra. These follow the rainbow colours.
Attribute: Each chakra has many attributes and associated organs in the body. For the purpose of this short summary, I have just provided the main attribute.
Body, Mind, Spirit: This is a quick summary of the main purification process for each of the three main bodies.
Negative agenda beings: The shadow side of the chakra[127].

---

[126] There are also the multidimensional chakras outside the body: 10th to 15th chakras, and two new chakras within the body (8th and 9th) but these have been excluded as at this moment as there are no personal purification processes needed for these chakras. They have not been polluted.

103

My Way Zen

One word summary: I came across this simplified phrase in Glastonbury[128] that characterises each chakra and included it here.

Shadow work: Suggested practices to clean up your "shadow".

Advanced: For each chakra, there is an advanced section, which has some ideas of a more advanced nature. If you would like more information about these, please contact me at **mywayzen@gmail.com.**

---

[127] Red Pill: Negative Agenda Beings i.e. the Dark side. There are many different groups. The main ones come from the Rothschilds and other banking families and the "blue bloods" and other Luciferian Zionists. Please contact the author for more details about the Negative Agenda Beings. I could write another book on these criminals. Suffice it to say that they have lost as they always do. There are now (Feb 2019) over 82,000 sealed indictments for those in the USA which will have to answer for their crimes against Humanity.

[128] The short phrases were in the menu for 7 smoothies at a restaurant in Glastonbury - the Excalibur.

1. Root Chakra - Survival

Original form of injunction	Promise not to kill or steal	Body	Healthy nutrition and good quality alkaline water
Location	Root or base of spine (perineum)	Mind	Overcoming fear
Indian name	Muladhara	Spirit	Forgiveness of our human failings
Colour	Red	Negative Agenda	Generation of fear
Attribute	Survival	Shadow work	Investigate your fears and go beyond them.
One word summary	I Am		

The purification process for the root chakra is mainly to do with the body - cleaning up what you eat i.e. good nutrition based on fresh organic alkaline foods filled with light. The purification process also includes reducing your meat consumption. Meat (and some fish) is one of the worse sources of toxins that we are currently eating. Not only is meat very acidic and filled with all sorts of pesticides, drugs and fear toxins, but also it is by far the most environmentally damaging activity that we humans are currently doing[129]. The

My Way Zen

purification process is to slowly adjust until you are vegan and perhaps even progressing to fruitarian and so on[130]. It also involves cleaning the digestive track (colonics) and cleaning the other organs such as the kidneys, gall bladder and liver. This path may also include regular fasts[131]. There are numerous books on nutrition. My favourites are

- Spiritual Nutrition by Dr Gabriel Cousens
- Thrive by Brendan Brazier
- River Cottage (vegetarian food) by Hugh Fearnley Whittingstall
- The Green Roasting Tin by Rukmini Iyer

The process of un-adaption to the toxicity of the normal western diet takes time. My advice is do not set unreasonable goals and do not rush the cleaning up process. Slowly remove items from your diet that are not healthy. The big one is meat. The meat industry, as currently configured, is horrendous and it is best not to participate in it. If you can find meat from animals that have lived and died in a humane way and were blessed, then maybe occasionally, if the body needs it, it may be appropriate to add some meat into your diet.

The purification of the body through an alkaline diet can be augmented by drinking alkaline water (i.e. water with a pH higher than 7.0). I have a Kangen water device that purifies and ionises the water and makes it alkaline (pH 8.5 to pH 9.5).

---

[129] For the information on this, please watch the Earthlings documentary film.

[130] Please see Hilton Hotema's books, particularly Man's Higher Consciousness, for explanation of the path to a fully clean diet.

[131] One source of dietary information that I follow is Thomas Dealer, who recommends that we break our fast as late as possible in the day - 2pm or even 4pm if you can last that long. Having a full English breakfast just after waking up is exactly the wrong thing to do!

Endocrine system

The endocrine system - the hypothalamus, pineal and pituitary gland, the pancreas, thyroid and adrenal glands are all hugely important to the healthy function of the human body. These all need major cleanups. One method I use is the Initiate U health meditation. I have included this on the My Way Zen website.

Innate and Self healing

Innate is the name given by Kryon to the intelligence of the body. Our human body is an amazing self-healing mechanism. Normally it can heal itself, but when the level of toxicity that accumulates in the body is too great, the natural self-healing ability of the body is overwhelmed, and we get diseases. One practice that I like to do is to talk to Innate (the body) You can help by encouraging it and ask what you need to do to assist it in healing the body. You will often get a clear message, which could be as simple as resting and let the body heal itself.

Mind and spirit

With regard to the mind and spirit aspects of the root chakra, my suggestions are to look at your fears. The root fear that I found was about survival, after all we are mortal will creatures. In my case, this root fear was overcome through the Template process[132]. This uses sacred geometry to connect up various circuits which have been disconnected. When these are re-connected, you will no longer worry about the future (or past), and you become free of Fear.

The negative agenda beings live off our fear. I believe the money system was designed to feed our fear, at a survival level. It is designed to have scarcity built in via usury. I could write a whole

---

[132] The Template website is www.thetemplateorg.com. The first ceremony (Original Innocence) and the second ceremony are both on youtube and can be activated for free at www.youtube.com/user/thetemplateorg

book about the money system. But for now, I will just say the old system is unsustainable and will, at some stage, collapse. This may be distressing for some people, but in the long run, the collapse of the existing greed based financial system will be a huge step forward in our ascension.

Forgiveness is the key to releasing your pain. Forgiveness is more about yourself than about other people. Forgiveness plays a huge role in the first ceremony of the Template, called Original Innocence. I was privileged to perform the ceremony a few years ago and it was during this that I lost my fear.

Shadow Work

Shadow work is perhaps the most challenging part of the purification process. It requires enormous courage to look within to find those parts of yourself that you do not like and have repressed as the Shadow. Carl Jung coined this term and the recommendation is to forgive yourself and withdraw your projections – the projection of your shadow onto others.

Advanced

H'oponopono practice - repeating and feeling through self-identification, the following words: "I am sorry, Please forgive me, I love you, Thank you."

Salts of Salvation – When our bodies are alkalinised and have each of the 12 salts of salvation, magical things can happen, according to Santos Bonacci. Please check our his youtube channel for details of the salts. As a reminder of the salts and which zodiac sign and part of the body they are linked to, I painted a picture of rainbow man based on the famous Vitruvian man by Leonardo da Vinci. I have called the picture Ecce Homo and I plan to write a book on its symbolism. It is presented below:

My Way Zen

Ecce Homo

2. Sacral Chakra - Creativity

Original form of injunction	Promise not to commit adultery	**Body**	Sacred sexual activity
Location	Middle of the hip region and sexual organs	**Mind**	Creative Genius
Indian name	Swadhisthana	**Spirit**	Forgiveness of sexual misconduct
Colour	Orange	**Negative Agenda**	Sexual perversion

Attribute	Creativity, including sexual activity	**Shadow work**	Be comfortable in your own skin, your body including your genitals
One word summary	I Feel		

This chakra has been polluted by sexual misconduct. Consequently, the clean-up process is to practice sacred sex and avoid impure sexual activity (whatever that means to you).

The negative agenda beings are the main culprits: - sexual perversion, paedophilia and "sex magic" is not acceptable and the criminals who have perpetrated these crimes will be brought to justice.

Mind and Spirit

The second chakra is the source of our creativity. The advice here is to follow your passions, what brings you joy and feeds your creativity. The process mirrors the fourth chakra, the Heart. Join these two chakras, the sacral and the heart at the spirit level and you become an unstoppable "force of nature".

Advanced

The advanced practice for this chakra is to connect this chakra to the Heart chakra and pineal gland via Tantric sex.

Alternatively, the advanced practice could be Chasity. My understanding Chastity as a Christian practice came from the book Mere Christianity by CS Lewis[133]. The idea is that married couples

My Way Zen

are joined together as "One flesh". During the early years of the marriage when the desire is to make babies, then be as lustful as possible. When this period has ended, then reduce sexual activity until you can reach the stage of celibacy. This stage is often thought of as chastity, but the original idea of chastity includes both phases. Make love when you really are in love. If you are not in love, it is best to abstain.

---

[133] CS Lewis was a contemporary of JRR Tolkien and wrote the Chronicles of Narnia.

3. Solar Plexus - Identity and Power

Original form of injunction	Promise not to serve any God other than the Most High	**Body**	Exercise and breath work. Fasting
Location	Around your naval area	**Mind**	Service to others
Indian name	Manipura	**Spirit**	Self discipline
Colour	Yellow	**Negative Agenda**	Narcissism to an extreme degree
Attribute	Identity and Personal Power	**Shadow work**	Humility
One word summary	I Do		

The main purification process for the third chakra is a move away from Power **without** i.e. power over others to Power **within** i.e. will power and self-discipline. This is the chakra that is even more polluted that the second chakra by false power systems and the idolisation of celebrity. The clean-up of this chakra involves deep seated humility.

For the body, daily exercise is recommended. This can be vigorous or could be just walking (preferably in Nature). Breathwork, such as Taoist breathing as practiced by Mantak Chia, including the inner smile practice, is recommended along with fasting and self-discipline.

Advanced

Who Am I? practice: This is a meditative practice where you look for your identity by asking the question "Who am I" repeatedly until you get an answer. It was one of Ramana Maharishi's favourite meditation practices.

4. Heart Chakra - Personal love and respect

Original form of injunction	Promise to respect your parents and Elders	**Body**	Be in Nature. Massage to heal trauma
Location	In the centre of the chest around your heart region	**Mind**	Find your Passion and live it
Indian name	Anahata	**Spirit**	Worship and self worth
Colour	Green	**Negative Agenda**	Psychopathic behaviour
Attribute	Love and relationships	**Shadow work**	Relationship work, including "cutting cords".
One word summary	I Love		

For me, this chakra needed a lot of purification. Our relationships nowadays are extremely complicated. We have numerous divorces

My Way Zen

and failed relationships (including myself). So we need to do the shadow work, heal the wounds, and cut the cords with old relationships that no longer serve. The injunction given by Jesus was Love your neighbour as yourself ("The Golden rule").

My suggestions are to spend as much time in Nature, in a natural environment in the woods, or by a sea, or in the mountains. All these heal the heart. The reason that Nature is so beneficial maybe that in nature there is no mind and it is free from electro-magnetic radiation (EMF)[134].

Each of us has a passion (or passions), it is what we love doing. The purification process is to feel your passion, by feeling joy. What brings you the most joy? The idea is to merge what you do, your work and so on, with your passion. If you need a permission slip[135] to take action, please refer to Bashar who regularly hands out permission slips.

When it comes to the Spirit, for me it becomes a heart felt "Praise the Lord" - a true feeling of worship, not a mechanistic repeating of words, rather a passionate Yes to life and to our Creator.

---

[134] If you can find a place without EMF radiation (no cell phone towers or electric pylons), all the better. EMF from mobile phones at the 4G is difficult for the brain to handle for any length of time. 5G is even worse. See Barrie Trower on youtube for more information on the dangers of 5G.

[135] According to Bashar, all tools, techniques, rituals and so on are basically permission slips, allowing you to break free of pre-programmed beliefs that act as obstacles. Just give yourself permission to be free of the obstacle and you are.

The Atheist dilemma or Ignorance.

Our ignorance, about ourselves, where we are from and where we are going, is profound. We can easily make mistakes. I am afraid atheists have made a big mistake. I can see how the word God can be easily misunderstood, perhaps as an old guy with a white beard sitting on a cloud. Of course, such an image is false and can be dispensed with. I prefer to use the word God-source, as it refers to the Creator or source of everything. There is a Creator as we are living in a virtual reality. The problem with denying the existence of God is that you can easily make the same mistake that Lucifer made.

Purification of the Heart chakra

The purification process is to become more loving in your relationships, particularly with your parents. The original form also included your elders, but due to dementia and Alzheimer's and other old age diseases, this injunction is not so relevant today, so I have left it out. I am over 60, I feel there is a place for seniors in society which is not currently seen nowadays. Perhaps the original form for this chakra which includes honour your elders could be included?

The Negative agenda beings seem to have a cold heart and don't seem to feel the same way we do. This leads to psychopathic behaviour. Ultimately, the truth will out and any criminal activities will be exposed for what they are.

Advanced

Self-love, self-worth, and self-validation are all key steps to be taken on the path to 5th Dimensional Unconditional Love. Now we enter Boundless openness and feel the full blessings from our God-source.

5. Throat chakra - Communication

Original form of injunction	Promise not to bear false witness	Body	Be authentic Singing or Toning
Location	Throat	Mind	Mindfulness or sitting in silence
Indian name	Vishudatha	Spirit	Breath work and Revocations
Colour	Blue	Negative Agenda	Lies and deception
Attribute	Communication	Shadow work	Walk in Beauty by cleaning up your expression in the world.
One word summary	I Speak		

Cleanup your words - to "walk in beauty", a shamanic description of being honest, with yourself and with others. This is the Age of Authenticity - one of the many names for the times we live in (see appendix 4.

The negative agenda or shadow side of this chakra is obviously lies and deception. Satan is known as the great deceiver. When you start the awakening process you begin to realise the extent of lies that we

116

are being told. It is staggering and it could be as much as 80 to 90% of what we think is true, turns out to be false: World History, Science, Health systems, the false claims of advertisers, religion and "gods", about food, 9/11 and 7th July bombings and so on.

Revocations - These are powerful declarations to be made in your own voice. I recommend those from Andrew Bartzis, The Galactic Historian whose latest program is Living the Mystical Life Daily. Words are powerful. Some people see words as spells, after all, spelling could be understood as using words as spells. I have recorded one of the revocations - the Shaman's Death and it is available for free on the MyWayZen website.

Advanced

The advanced practice is to adopt Radical Honesty[136].

Another advance practice could be singing or toning. The two that I like are: The Hu chant, an ancient spiritual practice brought up to date through Eckankar; and The OM Meditation, particularly the one with Buddha Maitreya the Christ. He has recorded many powerful shamanic type meditations such as the Coming Destiny, A Soul I Walk on Earth and As Many Atoms. All can be found at Shambhala Tools.

---

[136] The details of this very advanced practice is in a book called Radical Honesty - How to Transform your Life by telling the Truth by Brad Blanton.

6. Third eye chakra - Balance and sacred union

Original form of injunction	Not covered	**Body**	Activate the Pineal Gland
Location	Third Eye is located in the centre of the Brain around the pineal gland	**Mind**	Balance
Indian name	Anja	**Spirit**	Shamanic path
Colour	Violet/Indigo	**Negative Agenda**	Male domination and subjugation of the Female
Attribute	Psychic ability & access to hidden truths	**Shadow work**	Clean up karma and past life choices.
One word summary	I See		

The pineal gland is the secret portal where the most powerful and highest source of ethereal Divine energy is available to us. This is the centre of Illumination where our cosmic vision and divine knowing is initiated.

As this organ is so important to our humanity, it has been under attack by the Negative Agenda Beings. The biggest issue is fluoride

My Way Zen

which calcifies the pineal. In order to activate the pineal, my recommendations are:

- Drink unfloridated spring water
- Eat foods that enhance the pineal (see online)
- Sacred ceremony - psychoactive entheogens.
- Meditation and transmissions can be used. My favourite is the one by the Children of the Sun, Pineal Activation[137].

This chakra is about balancing the brain. The brain has two halves and tends to operate in a polarised, dualistic way. After resolving the lower chakras, it is time to start the healing process of the higher chakras including Third Eye chakra. I have been helped by the shamanic practices here of altered states, including Ayahusca.

Balance

From the point of view of Duality, there is Good and Bad, Black and White, High and Low etc. at this level of understanding there is a beautiful natural process of prey/predator keeping everything in balance.

Advanced

An advanced practice is Hieros Gamos, the sacred wedding of Male and Female. In order to accomplish this, you need to find and express both the male and female aspects within yourself. It is a balancing of genders to attain the next level of consciousness – the angelic perspective.

7. Crown chakra - Divine Intuition or Knowing

---

[137] See My Way Zen website for this activation transmission from Children of the Sun.

My Way Zen

Original form of injunction	Not covered	Body	Sitting (Zazen). Microcosmic circle
Location	Top of your head	Mind	Mercy, forgiveness, wisdom and compassion.
Indian name	Sahasrara	Spirit	Surrender to the Will of God.
Colour	White	Negative Agenda	Luciferian and Satanic practices
Attribute	Divine Knowing or Gnosis	Shadow work	None
One word summary	I Know		

This chakra is about connecting with the Divine and surrendering to the Will of God. The way we are currently configured, we can make mistakes, when you try to intuit the Will of God. Although when you really get it, there are no mistakes. We can misunderstand what is the will of God. Divine Intuition (or Gnosis) is only available at the later stages of the path when the lower chakras are purified, and you begin to see clearly. My advice is to start with the lower chakras first. When these are clean, then work on the higher chakras, specifically avoid anything above the throat chakra, other than meditation.

For the body, the purification process is meditation and silent

My Way Zen

centring prayer. In Zen, it is just sitting (Zazen). It also includes contemplation and studying sacred scriptures. You can also try the micro cosmic circuit[138]. You take a conscious breath in and out forming a circle within the body with the tongue placed in a special position.

I also recommend what I call kingship (or queenship if there is a female version of becoming a sovereign being). If you are ready and willing to take 100% responsibility for you and your actions, you can become a citizen of One Earth Nation[139].

The negative agenda beings follow Luciferian or Satanic practices. I don't want to report on this as firstly, I have not been to any of their meetings, so I don't have first hand evidence. I have heard testimony of whistle blowers such as one of the daughters of the Rothschilds. It is completely disgusting and the beings that perform these blood rituals need to be exposed and dealt with appropriately.

Advanced

Use Shambhala Healing Tools. Please write to the author at **MyWayZen@gmail.com** if you want more information about Shambhala.

Seven Rays

In the spirit of completeness, I have included the table below. This shows the healthy alignment of the chakras with the seven rays. This is a complicated teaching given by Djwhal Khul. In summary, we have an unhealthy ray package where the 5th, 7th and 4th rays are located in the Root, Third Eye, and Sacral chakras respectively.

---

[138] I received the explanation of the micro cosmic circuit from Ken Wilber. It is one of his main practices in the Superhuman V2.0 operating system.

[139] One Earth Nation is in the process of being set up. Its website is at onearthnation.one.

The healing process is to align the rays with the healthy version shown below:

Chakra	Attribute	Healthy version
• Root chakra	Survival	4th Ray of Harmony through conflict
• Sacral chakra	Creativity	7th Ray of Sacred Ceremony
• Solar Plexus	Power & Identity	6th Ray of Devotion
• Heart chakra	Love & Respect	2nd Ray of Loving Wisdom
• Throat chakra	Communication	3rd Ray of Abstract Intelligence
• Third Eye	Balance	5th Ray of Concrete Knowledge
• Crown chakra	Divine Intuition	1st Ray of Will & Power

My Way Zen

There are numerous books explaining the chakras, their colours, sounds and so forth. Please do your own investigation. The practical applications of the chakra system, I have used are:

1. The ACE Evolutionary spiral chakra meditation by Barbara Marx Hubbard and the Quantum Powers online course with Jean Houston. I qualified as an Agent of Conscious Evolution (ACE) many years ago when Barbara Marx Hubbard gave an amazing online course in preparation for 2012. I recorded the Evolutionary chakra meditation and a free download can be found on the My Way Zen website.[140]

2. The Quantum Powers course with Jean Houston was also very powerful. There is a process associated with each of the chakras:

- Quantum Self
- Orchestrate Time
- Power of the Quantum mind
- Manifestation
- Healing and endless energy
- Unique Genius

There are numerous formulations of the purification process. The two that I have followed are the Seven Steps to Heaven (by David Boyle) and the Divine Keys from the Innerversity of Divine Perfection (IODP).

---

[140] Details of these resources are on the My Way Zen website (Appendix I).

Chakras

Please note that there are hundreds of chakras in the body, including those in the feet and in the hands, all over the head and so on. The subtle energy body has many meridians where the life energy flows. A nexus is formed where these cross. This is called a chakra in the ancient Indian systems as it looks like a whirling vortex or wheel of energy (if you can see the subtle energy body). While there are hundreds of chakras, there are currently seven main ones in the body, although some systems use 6 or even 8 or 9. It does not really matter as these are just maps of the subtle energy body. For purposes of this book I have used the seven chakra system as this is the most common one.

Advanced

When our DNA is activated, we will have access to many more chakras which are outside the body, such as the Earth Star chakra underneath the feet which connects you to the Planet. There are also various higher chakras that connects you to the Sun and to the rest of the Universe. In addition, some of the chakras within the body may merge as part of the Ascension process. The three lower chakras (Root, Sacral and Solar Plexus) merge into a single chakra directly connected to the Heart chakra which is joined by the Krystos chakra (The higher heart). These are all coming on line as our DNA is activated. So, anything is possible.

Ultimate energy clearing protocol

My dear brother, Christof Melchizedek, is offering a quick way of cleaning up our energy field with the Ultimate energy clearing protocol. It covers a lot of the shadow work noted above in the My Way Zen purification process and it is thoroughly recommended. It includes:

My Way Zen

1. Clearing imprinted programs
2. Soul longings
3. Karma cleaning and cleaning past life choices
4. Soul level contracts cleaned up
5. Inorganic material removed from your energy field
and many more purification processes. Please check

The Pineal Induction technique and the associated codes and tones are available from the My Way Zen website. The two codes featured are the Centreness key and the Guardian Code. There are numerous other codes such as

- Hieros Gamos
- Hypercube
- Eye of Karma
- Krystal star TriWave
- Genesis Cells rebirth
- Plasma Flame
- Morphogenetic Plasma
- Imprint Removal
- Chakra Bio-Restructure
- Christos Revival
- Crown Repair
- Excalibur
- Superabundance
- 8 genesis cell code

Appendix 6 – Awakening

Awakening can have many meanings. For me, the first stage was a spiritual awakening. This meaning of awakening is waking up to who you are.

Then for me, the next stage was waking up to the Deep State "dominate and control system" and who is behind it. The process of waking up is different for different people (the My Way Zen perspective). The important thing is to Wake Up.

Three awakening puzzles were set in chapter 1. There were:

- 9/11 – Is the official story of the "terrorist" attack on the Twin Towers true?
- Pyramids - were they just tombs for deceased Pharaohs?
- Why do we have 46 chromosomes, but other simians (apes) have 48, i.e. does the Darwinian evolution theory explain the source of our DNA?

My answers, after many years of research are set out below. As always, please do you own research.

1. The 9/11 event was a False Flag[141] event carried out by the Deep State for their own nefarious reasons. This event includes the controlled demolition of building seven and the rocket attack on the Pentagon.
2. The Giza pyramids were built as an energy and ascension

---

[141] From Wiki: A false flag is a covert operation designed to deceive; the deception creates the appearance of a particular party, group, or nation being responsible for some activity, disguising the actual source of responsibility.

My Way Zen

machine by various ET beings, possibly under the direction of Ra or Thoth using advanced technology many thousands of years ago. There is no evidence that they were built as tombs for Pharaohs using blocks and tackle by a huge primitive workforce.

3. Our DNA was seeded on this planet by ET beings who were master geneticists. Our human DNA is an amalgamation of DNA from many ET races. It has been manipulated and that is why we only have 46 chromosomes.

Appendix 7 – The Urantia Book

The Urantia Book is new revelation about the mysteries of God, the Universe, world history, Jesus and ourselves. It consists of 196 papers (2,097 pages), split into 4 parts:

Part I - The Central and Super Universes (there are seven super universes)
Part II - The Local Universe (which is called Nebadon)
Part III - The History of Urantia (Urantia is the name for the planet we call Earth)
Part IV - The Life and Teachings of Jesus (This is perhaps the most interesting section of the book).

I am still reading and absorbing the information contained in this amazing book. It makes a lot of sense, but I am not 100% convinced as there appears to be quite a bit missing. However, it presents what I feel is the most comprehensive cosmology and theology that we have currently available.

It was revealed to the "contact group" in the 1920s and 1930s in Chicago, but the book was not published until 1955.

If reading the 2000+ pages is a bit daunting, you can download individual papers for free. In addition, each paper has been made into an audio file which can also be downloaded for free.

My favourite source of information about the book is Bryon Belitsos, mainly because he also brings in subsequent revelations, called the Teaching Mission. Some "Urantiaists" have become dogmatic and say that only the material from the original book can be used. My view is that things have moved on from the 1920s and 1930s and so I would like to include the new information.

The Urantia book covers a huge amount of information, so I can only draw out in this book the key elements.

The Divine Plan

There is a Divine Plan for the evolution of intelligent life on inhabited planets. This plan has been followed millions of times and it works. However, one very clever and brilliant angel thought he could do better. He was called Lucifer. He argued that as we have never seen the Creator God, such a being does not exist. The Universal Father, who dwells in Paradise, has delegated everything He can delegate to His "Paradise Sons". The Paradise Son that is now the supreme ruler of our local Universe is called Christ Michael. In order to become the supreme ruler of a universe, the Paradise Son has to take seven bestowals (i.e. incarnate as one of his creatures). The final bestowal of Christ Michael was on Urantia as Jesus. There is a very interesting account of his life and teachings in Part IV which I believe is a must read for anybody interested in this great man.

Lucifer rebellion and the two defaults

Lucifer rebelled 200,000 years ago and our planetary prince at the time, who was called Caligastia, joined the rebellion along with over 30 other planets. This was a key factor in the first default. The Divine plan for evolution is that when a planet is ready, it will receive human DNA. When this has evolved sufficiently, the next major stage is for the planetary prince to set up a large capital city of at least 500,000 human beings. When this has been established, an Adam and Eve incarnates on the planet. They have advanced DNA and by mating with the best of the local humans, we get a huge uplift in our physical and mental abilities.

So, what happened on Urantia? Caligastia did make the initial visit

My Way Zen

500,000 years ago, along with 100 of his angelic staff (this group sound very like the Anunnaki). 200,000 years ago, Caligastia and over half of his staff joined the Lucifer rebellion. The capital city was not created so when Adam and Eve arrived 36,000 years ago, in the first Eden possibly somewhere near Cyprus[142], they had a very difficult time. The second default arose as Eve mated with another group of human hybrids (the Nodites). These were off spring from the Caligastia group who had mated with local humans, despite being specifically ordered not to do this - see Book of Enoch for details. These human hybrids were probably the giants, or the mighty men of renown mentioned in the Bible.

So, we now have two defaults and a planet that is significantly out of alignment with the Divine plan. Christ Michael (Jesus) by his life and actions has started the process that will bring us back in line. The key step was the release of the Spirit of Truth at Pentecost (which he could only do after dying and being resurrected in his morontia body). If you want to know more about this, I recommend reading the book - or at least Part IV.

This is where the main book ends its story. The Teaching Mission continues the story with the Lucifer Adjudication. This has been completed and Lucifer chose to be uncreated. All records and timelines had to be adjusted as if Lucifer did not exist. It is always a huge event when an uncreation happens as many lives can be effected.

We are now in the Correcting Time and the next step will be the Magisterial Mission. The Paradise Son that will be in charge of this process is called Manjoronson.

---

[142] The first Eden (translated as garden in the Bible) could be the Atlantis. This area is now underwater, so it is difficult to determine exactly where Atlantis was located.

Magisterial Mission

I believe that the Urantia Book, along with the Teaching Mission, provides one of the best explanations of the issues we face on Urantia (Earth) and what to do about it. Basically, it is all in hand. It is not our job to judge anyone. The Judgment will be carried out by the Magisterial Mission, who are extremely experienced in such matters. Of course, nobody can predict when this will happen (the day of judgement) and what the result will be. All I know for sure is that we have a loving father in Paradise who wants the very best for us.

Planet of the Cross

Urantia has become a bit of a celebrity in the Universe, not least because the supreme ruler of our universe, Christ Michael, took his last bestowal here and has promised to return. We are known as the planet of the Cross. The Melchizedeks have played a significant role in the affairs of Urantia, including the intervention by Machiventa Melchizedek approximately two millennia before the birth of Jesus.

Cosmology

The Urantia Book contains a massive amount of information on the structure of the cosmos. Here is a brief summary:

Cosmos	Name	Comments
Earth	Urantia	Our planet
Solar System	Monmatia	
Local system	Satania	Capital = Jerusem
Local constellation	Norlatiadek	Capital = Edentia

My Way Zen

Local Universe	Nebadon	Capital = Salvington
Super Universe	Orvonton	Capital = Uversa
Central universe	Havona	Central island = Paradise

Our planet number within the local system is 606. This ties in with another source that says our galactic number is 853/847024/606, which is an interesting tie in.

There are thousands of universes within a super universe. There are seven super universes. The one we are in, Orvonton, is the seventh.

Christ Michael

Christ Michael is the name of the supreme ruler of this Universe, the "Logos". In order to become the supreme ruler a paradise son needs to take seven bestowals (or incarnations). For his final bestowal Christ Michael chose Urantia (i.e. this planet). So, look into the skies and understand that we are in a very small part of one spiral in an average galaxy called the Milky Way (or Norlatiadek) and then as far as the Hubble Telescope can see there are millions of galaxies, each with billions of stars and planets, lots of which are inhabited by intelligent life as life is everywhere. This is our local universe. The supreme ruler of this entire Universe chose this planet for his final bestowal. Christ Michael is number 611,211 of Paradise sons, so this indicates that there are many thousands of other local universes. It all gets a bit mind blowing at this stage.

Christ Michael took incarnation as Jesus in 7BC (our calendar is slightly out of sync).

Jesus Mission

According to the Urantia book the main mission of Jesus was

completed during the 40 days in the wilderness on Mt Hebron (modern day Syria), when he successfully deposed Caligastia as planetary prince and took on that role himself. This ended the rebellion status of Urantia. He could have ended his bestowal then, but he decided to continue his life on Urantia. He gathered together the disciples and started the teaching mission, which is covered in part in the gospels. The Urantia Book explains who actually wrote the gospels and when they were written.

Missing aspects in the Urantia Book

While I am new reader of the Urantia Book, I have found it to be full of information that resonates with me. Whether it is true or not is up to you to determine. I was a bit disappointed that some of my pet theories are not in the book. The ones that I would have liked to have seen, was more information about Mary Magdalene. In some teachings, she is represented as equal to Jesus, but the Urantia book hardly mentions her. The other one is the local tradition[143] that Jesus visited Glastonbury in England with his uncle Joseph of Arimathea who operated a tin transport business[144]. Jesus could easily have made the journey with him. While the Urantia book covers each year of the life of Jesus, it does not mention a trip to England. There are perhaps other big omissions. Krishna is not mentioned at all in the Urantia Book. Neither is Sananda[145]. It also does not deal with the Jewish problem[146] perhaps because this is

---

[143] Maybe this was the source of William Blakes's great poem Jerusalem - "And did those feet walk upon ." See Appendix 11 for the full poem, which I believe is England's true national anthem.

[144] The tin business in England was principally located in Cornwall and the west country. The tin was collected centrally, and boats transported it across the English Channel to France and then across the Mediterranean to the Roman empire.

[145] Sananda is the name used for the Ascended Master who took the form of Jesus, according to some people.

My Way Zen

too sensitive a topic. The other area missing from the Urantia Book is an explanation of the different racial types of the extra-terrestrial visitors. For example was Caligastia reptilian?

---

[146] Please see the Book of Revelations 2:9: 'I know your tribulation and your poverty (but you are rich) and the slander of those who say that they are Jews and are not but are a synagogue of Satan'.

My Way Zen

Appendix 8 – Four Bodhisattva vows

The wording of the four bodhisattva vows shown below comes from the Wild Goose Sangha[147].

Sentient beings are numberless, I vow to save them.
Desires are inexhaustible, I vow to put an end to them.
The Dharmas are boundless, I vow to master them
The Buddha way is unattainable, I vow to attain it.

Understood in a conventional way, these vows seem paradoxical or even non-sensical. With the My Way Zen perspective that we are in a Q♀VR, I am able to make sense of these vows. Here is my best shot at trying to explain the unexplainable.

Sentient beings are numberless, I vow to save them: The realisation is that, at a profound level all is perfect. We are part of the Divinely created world within pure consciousness. Consequently, there is nothing to save.

Desires are inexhaustible, I vow to put an end to them: When you enter the Holy of Holies, the sacred neutral, deep within your heart, to a place of self love and forgiveness, you discover you have no desires. So even though they are inexhaustible, you can go to a place where desires have ended.

The Dharmas are boundless, I vow to master them: Dharmas generally refers to knowledge, books, realisations, teachings and so on. This vow is perhaps the most difficult of the four vows to

---

[147] Wild Goose Sangha is the Zen sangha that I belong to.

My Way Zen

achieve as it means total self-mastery. However, recognising that within a virtual reality, there are some things that will always remain a mystery, you begin to realise that you know very little and what you think you know, may be false. As Socrates said, "True wisdom comes from knowing that you know nothing".

If you look very carefully at anything - a tree, or a bird or anything, you realise that you don't really know anything. Of course, you can give a tree a name, but this does not mean that you know the tree. The place to be is in Surrender, Surrender to the Mystery. To Surrender as a Master means a complete Surrender to the Will of God. This is how you master the Dharmas.

The Buddha way is unattainable, I vow to attain it: This is perhaps the most enigmatic of the four vows. As any Zen practitioner knows, it is impossible to explain how the Way is attained. No work, books or courses can do the job. The only way is to experience it. This is the attainment.

My Way Zen

Appendix 9 – Jesus, the Mystery

As the Great Master, Jesus figures a lot in this book and there appears to be a lot of speculation in the spiritual circles about Jesus (or Sananda / Christ Michael), I have added this section on the Mystery of Jesus. Firstly, let us make it clear Jesus was a Jew and not a Christian. I believe he did not plan to create a religion that worships him. He was a human being, but a very special one. I believe he was crucified, and he did die on the cross.

The revelations in the Urantia Book contains the best account of his life and teachings that I have read. Every year of his life is covered in detail. The description of his teaching mission, crucifixion, resurrection and ascension are all described in such detail, it is as if they were observed, perhaps by angels and other invisible beings.

Subsequent to his life, many stories and misunderstandings have arisen, not least among his disciples, some of who were heavily bought into the idea of a Messiah, a saviour for the Jewish people and gentiles. Jesus said he was not the Messiah, but it became such a difficult area that he stopped answering the question "Are you the Messiah?" and just said "those words are yours."

His denial that he was the Messiah, the secret longing of the Jews for someone to re-establish the Kingdom of the Jews, may have upset many of the close friends and family of Jesus, including his mother and family. It was perhaps the main reason for the betrayal by Judas. This is all explained in the Urantia Book.

Personal search

I have been privileged to travel to many sacred sites in 2016 and

2017 to complete a complicated series of activations. The journey started with Table Mountain (South Africa), Arunachala (India), Mt Rayner (Seattle, USA), Mont Blanc, via Uluru in Australia and Mt Huashan in China. I ended up in Israel - Jerusalem to determine whether Jesus was buried at the Church of the Holy Sepulchre. The answer I got was "no". I also went to the Garden tomb just outside the Damascus gate. I also got a "no" there as well. So, I headed to Kashmir to Roza Bal tomb in Srinagar as there is a claim made that the ascended Jesus travelled to the Himalayas and left his body at Srinagar. I checked this out as well and again received a "no". So, at the end of my travels, I came to the view that Jesus did not leave a body behind on Urantia[148]. He really is a mystery.

The Paradox

Apparently, there have been time travellers who have been able to time travel to the past and somehow changed the timelines. One of the big dangers with time travel is that paradoxes can be created[149]. Most of these are not too big and can be resolved by the time correction program. However, some are so enormous they have caused major problems with our timelines and ascension process. I have heard that there are 4 of these fundamental paradoxes - I don't know exactly what they are, but my guess is that the stories of Jesus is one of the paradoxes. There are so many stories now that challenge the traditional story in our religions e.g. Did he die on the cross? or was he revived after spending only a short time (c3hrs) on the cross? - in which case there was no resurrection. Such puzzles are best left to history.

---

[148] This ties in with the 3D images of the Turin Shroud which shows the body of Jesus floating just before it was returned to dust well-nigh instantaneously (according to the Urantia Book paper 189:section 3).

[149] One change to the timelines that is fairly well known is the Mandela effect. We can remember both Mandela dying in jail in the 1980s and then Mandela being released in 1990.

My Way Zen

My Way Zen

Appendix 10 – Pole Shifts

Gregg Braden[150] says the magnetics of the Earth have changed 14 times in the past 4.5 million years. Is it possible the GSF facilitated these changes? If so, then we may have a point to "date" the past events and predict the next GSF.

Short-term magnetic field reversals, called geomagnetic excursions, last a few thousand years, when Earth's geomagnetic field weakens dramatically.

Radioactive material embedded in ice cores revealed such events between 39,000 and 41,000 years ago (Laschamp excursion), and a 1,200-year event 32,000 to 34,000 years ago (Mono Lake excursion). The ice core showed the Northern Hemisphere briefly emerged from the last ice age some 14,700 years ago with a 22-degree-Fahrenheit spike in just 50 years, then plunged back into icy conditions before abruptly warming again about 11,700 years ago.

This is a complicated subject with many different views. Please refer to the experts in this field: Immanuel Velikovsky (Worlds in Collision) and Charles Hapgood (The Path of the Pole)[151], also there is a lot of information about Pole Shifts and the changes to the Schumann Resonance on the web. I am not sure if these are connected with the GSF or whether they can help with predicting when the GSF will occur. Both topics are worth investigating so that you can make up your own mind about the predictions of

---

[150] Gregg Braden is another of my heroes. He wrote about magnetic field changes and pole shifts a long time ago in Zero Point. One of his many recommendations is to join others in the Global Coherence Initiative.

[151] Alternatively you can get an idea of the different views by reading Pole Shifts by John White.

My Way Zen

major changes in the Earth.

The predicted pole shifts or magnetic field changes could be at an etheric level. Under this interpretation, they would only have an effect on our consciousness and not the 3D world (i.e. the virtual reality).

Appendix 11 – Poems

A World of Light

A poem by Elizabeth Jennings

Yes when the dark withdrew I suffered light
And saw the candles heave beneath the wax,
I watched the shadow of my old self dwindle
   As softly on my recollection stole
A mood the senses could not touch or damage,
A sense of peace beyond the breathing word.

   Day dawdled at my elbow. It was night
Within. I saw my hands, their soft dark backs
Keeping me from the noise outside. The candle
   Seemed snuffed into a deep and silent pool:
It drew no shadow round my constant image
For in a dazzling dark my spirit stirred.

   But still I questioned it. My inward sight
Still knew the senses and the senses' tracks,
I felt my flesh and clothes, a rubbing sandal,
   And distant voices wishing to console.
My mind was keen to understand and rummage
To find assurance in the sounds I heard.

My Way Zen

Then senses ceased and thoughts were driven quite
Away (no act of mine). I could relax
And feel a fire no earnest prayer can kindle;
Old parts of peace dissolved into a whole
And like a bright thing proud in its new plumage
My mind was keen as an attentive bird.

Yes fire, light, air, birds, wax, the sun's own height
I draw from now, but every image breaks.
Only a child's simplicity can handle
Such moments when the hottest fire feels cool,
And every breath is like a sudden homage
To peace that penetrates and is not feared.

Jerusalem

By William Blake

And did those feet in ancient time
Walk upon Englands mountains green:
And was the holy Lamb of God,
On Englands pleasant pastures seen!

And did the Countenance Divine,
Shine forth upon our clouded hills?
And was Jerusalem builded here,
Among these dark Satanic Mills?

Bring me my Bow of burning gold:
Bring me my arrows of desire:
Bring me my Spear: O clouds unfold!
Bring me my Chariot of fire!

I will not cease from Mental Fight,

My Way Zen

Nor shall my sword sleep in my hand:
Till we have built Jerusalem,
In Englands green & pleasant Land.

A poem by Rumi

English version by Andrew Harvey

The grapes of my body can only become wine
After the winemaker tramples me.
I surrender my spirit like grapes to his trampling
So my inmost heart can blaze and dance with joy.
Although the grapes go on weeping blood and sobbing
"I cannot bear any more anguish, any more cruelty"
The trampler stuffs cotton in his ears: "I am not working in ignorance
You can deny me if you want, you have every excuse,
But it is I who am the Master of this Work.
And when through my Passion you reach Perfection,
You will never be done praising my name.

Appendix 12 – Diamond Light

The Summer Solstice and the whole of June 2018 was a very special time. We have been gifted with another wave of plasmic light energy from the Sun. This wave was called the Diamond Wave. It means that we are receiving the highest frequencies that we have ever experienced on this planet. The Diamond light contains within all the other frequencies and appears as intense bright light.

The diamond light contains the codes for the Divine Mind of Perfection[152].

Light	5th dim Solar Aspects of deity
Sapphire Blue	God's Will, Illumined Faith, Power, Protection, and God's First Cause of Perfection.
Sunshine Yellow	Christ Consciousness, Enlightenment, Wisdom, Illumination, Understanding, Perception, and Constancy
Crystalline Pink	Transfiguring Divine Love, Adoration, Tolerance, Oneness, and Reverence for ALL Life
White	The Immaculate Concept, Purity, Hope, Restoration, Resurrection and Ascension
Emerald Green	Illumined Truth, Healing, Consecration, Concentration, and Inner Vision.

---

[152] This table is a summary of the transmissions of the Diamond light by Patricia Cota Robles on Era of Peace, for example vlog 68.

My Way Zen

Light	5th dim Solar Aspects of deity
Ruby-Gold	**Divine Grace, Healing, Devotional Worship, Peace, and the Manifestation of the Christ**
Violet	**Mercy, Compassion, Forgiveness, Transmutation, Liberty, Justice, Freedom, Victory, and God's Infinite Perfection.**
Aquamarine	Clarity, Divine Perception, and Discernment.
Magenta	Harmony, Balance, Assurance, and God Confidence.
Gold	Eternal Peace, Prosperity, Abundance, and the God Supply of ALL Good Things.
Peach	Divine Purpose, Enthusiasm, and Joy
Opal*	Transformation and Transfiguration.

* Opalescent light is a new colour of iridescent light that was previously outside our visible light spectrum.

My Way Zen

Appendix 13 – The Quest for the Holy Grail

The following is from a dear friend of mine, An Ra Nae. In this short piece, she perfectly summarises the main import of this book - the journey hOMe.

The Journey of Life is the Quest to find the Holy Grail within. Your soul is programmed to return Home to the vibrational frequency of the God/Goddess that you are as the I AM Presence. It is this Sacred Journey, that is referred to as The Path, and that I call The Great Remembering.

The Quest for the Holy Grail is the innate desire of the Soul within each of us to reunite with God/Goddess within. It is the compelling force within us that has led people to undertake the arduous and sometimes lengthy pilgrimages to sacred temples throughout the ages.

It is the feeling that something is missing from your life and the longing for something more, even when all your outer needs are met. It is the still small voice within you urging you to follow the bread crumbs, the hints, the clues and urgings that if you say YES, it will take you all the way Home.

This Remembering is the dismantling of the human ego bit by bit and the surrendering to the Divine Will and Divine Plan of your sacred contract with life.

It is the willingness to follow your inner promptings and courageously follow that next YES, overcoming the fears, doubts and opposition from within and without.

It is the Path of Initiation that takes you to your own authenticity, empowerment and fulfilment of your Divine Plan.

My Way Zen

Appendix 14 – Source Declaration

The Source declaration is:
"I declare it is my intention to serve my God-Source with my full divine power, absolutely, unconditionally, completely. I am whole, I am sovereign, I am free".[153]

I have provided the following explanation for this powerful declaration, but the words speak for themselves.

Explanation

Source Declaration	Comments
I declare	Words have power. Spell the spelling.
it is my intention	My will is
to serve my God-Source	Your God-Source is referring to the source of your being, your Higher Self that dwells in the base reality. You surrender to the Will of God, to the Universal Father. It can be called the Shaman's death as you give up all attachments for the world and yourself as a separate being and become One with the entire system.
with my full divine power absolutely, unconditionally,	This is like the maximum effort of the black belt training (see Chapter 4).

---

[153] This is the old version of the Source Declaration. It was updated by Sananda and Shekinah to "I am Whole, I am Love, I am Divine". Use whichever version you prefer.

My Way Zen

Source Declaration	Comments
completely	
I Am Whole	This is Unity Consciousness. There is "no other". It is all one magnificent Virtual Reality
I Am Sovereign	For this to make sense, you need to know who the I Am is, the one that is the subject of the declaration. It is the I Am that is One with the Higher Self. It is not the Ego mind.

This is very important. If you don't understand this, you can fall in the trap that Lucifer fell into. Lucifer thought that there was no Higher Self, no higher authority. So, he thought his lower self, his ego mind was sovereign. |
| **I Am Free** | I Am Free means that you are free to become the servant of the Divine within you. This can seem paradoxical. True liberation is to give up all of the freedom of the lower mind and bring it 100% under the will of the Great I Am. |

My Way Zen

Index

A

Andrew Bartzis 27, 118
Andrew Cohen 21, 72
artificial intelligence 34, 40, 92
Ascension3, 5, 38, 45, 47, 49, 50, 54, 62, 69, 71, 74, 75, 76, 79, 80, 81, 82, 87, 92, 95, 96, 103, 145

B

Big TOE ....See *Theory of Everything*
Billy Carson 30

C

Carl Jung 15
Christianity 4, 6, 13, 14, 50, 57, 112
consciousness4, 6, 16, 18, 19, 21, 29, 31, 32, 36, 55, 58, 62, 69, 70, 71, 73, 74, 79, 82, 83, 86, 88, 89, 136, 141
Corey Goode 7, 40, 43, 49
coronal mass ejection ....See *Great Solar Flash*
Cosmic Disclosure 7, 40

D

David Icke...30
David Wilcock 5, 7, 42, 45, 94, 95
Deep State...49, 50, 82, 127
Dolores Cannon 48

E

Ekpyrosis 50
Emerald Tablets 30
Evolutionary Spirituality 21, 22, 72

F

False Flag...127

G

Gaia 6, 7, 40, 45, 49, 52, 53
Gaia TV 7, 40, 45, 49, 52

151

My Way Zen

Geshe Kelsang Gyatso..83
Gnostic texts..30
Golden Age..71, 78, 95, 103
Great Solar Flash 3, 7, 38, 39, 42, 43, 44
GSF 3, 41, 43, 44, 45, 49, 50, 54, 55, 140

H

Harvest 46, 47, 48, 50, 79
Holographic Universe 20

I

IODP..32, 33, 69, 94, 124

J

Janet Abels..4, 95
Jesus4, 5, 14, 31, 59, 60, 64, 72, 75, 76, 78, 81, 87, 88, 99, 115, 129, 130, 131, 132, 133, 134, 138, 139

L

Law of One 46, 79, 94

M

Main Stream Media 44
Making Zen your Own 5, 85, 95
Making Zen Your Own 4
Mary Magdalene..134
materialism 19
Matt Damon..22
Melchizedek Covenant 14, 55, 56, 57, 64, 81, 99
Mitch Batros..46
Mitch Battros..38
MMORG 18, 22, 36
My Way Zen1, 2, 4, 5, 14, 18, 25, 27, 41, 50, 55, 61, 64, 69, 75, 80, 83, 95, 98, 104, 108, 120, 124, 125, 126, 136

N

Nassim Haramein 22, 23
Negative Agenda Beings 39, 81, 82, 105, 119
Neil Bostrum..22
New Earth..6, 49, 103
non-physical reality..38
nPR See *non-physical reality*

My Way Zen

O

Oneness University 4

P

physicalism ....See *materialism*
Prof Nick Bostrom..34

Q

quantum physics...19
Quantum physics..22

R

Ra   46, 79, 95, 128, 147
Red Pill 39, 105
Rev Chris Collingwood 6

S

Source Field Investigations 5, 95
Spiral Dynamics..29
superintelligence...40, 92

T

The Matrix...20
The Signal 40
Theory of Everything 19, 21, 93
Tom Campbell 19, 24, 29, 32, 36, 38, 58, 93
Transcendental Meditation 4, 25

U

Unique Self...13, 14, 15, 90
Urantia Book.......5, 35, 36, 37, 56, 58, 60, 76, 77, 78, 81, 86, 87, 93, 99, 100, 129, 132, 134, 138

V

Virtual Reality 18, 19, 23, 25, 32, 36, 57, 82, 149

Z

Zen Buddhism 4

Printed in Great Britain
by Amazon